WORDS IN THE DUST

HOW JESUS SET ME FREE BY REDEEMING MY PAST

"I was riveted reading Sarah's story. It is refreshingly raw and vulnerable. In it, I saw the God of grace searching to redeem, cleanse, and deliver all from those covered areas in our hearts. As she states, 'Even when you aren't able to run to Him, He will still come running to you.'"

—ERIC GILMOUR, Founder of Sonship International

"My wife, Stefanie, and I are so proud of Sarah and her newest book, *Words in the Dust*. The thing that I love the most about *Words in the Dust* is how Sarah takes you on a journey of transparency that keeps you wanting to turn the page to find out what happened next. As you read through *Words in the Dust*, you may deeply relate to Sarah's story, and my prayer for you is that the Holy Spirit will draw you closer to Jesus and that His love and mercy will guide you. I believe that this book holds practical keys to return to God in the midst of hurt and pain. If you need a fresh start and a glimmer of hope, take time to read *Words in the Dust*."

—CHRIS OVERSTREET, Founder of Compassion to Action

"Sarah tells her personal testimony in such a beautiful and compelling way. Her story illustrates the journey of a young woman searching for her worth and value until she finds it in the arms of a loving Heavenly Father. It's a wonderful book. You won't want to put it down!"

—STEFANIE OVERSTREET

"Sarah is a pure heart with holy motivation to see those who feel lost and alone receive back their God-given voices and live the lives they were always destined to live. Despite your experience or your current season, this book will encourage you with honest reflections from Sarah's heart and her life story. It is an honor to know her and this book reflects the courage she carries into everything she does."

—JAKE HAMILTON, Founder of TheFIGHT
    Co-Founder of OneFlesh

"We absolutely love Sarah and the beautiful redemptive love story that God has written in her life. Sarah shares from a place of vulnerability that is so rare. The simple revelation of God's goodness, grace, and transforming love stirs hunger as a reader. If you are feeling hopeless, unworthy, or rejected, you need to read this book. There is freedom waiting for you. Healing is a person, and His name is Jesus. He's calling you home."

—WILLIAM & EMILY HINN, Senior Pastors
    Risen Nation Church

WORDS
IN
THE
DUST

HOW JESUS SET ME FREE BY
REDEEMING MY PAST

SARAH LORENTE

HIGH BRIDGE BOOKS
HOUSTON

It has been said, "The world needs dreamers and the world needs doers. But above all, the world needs dreamers that do." I have been a dreamer my entire life. I have dreamed of the impossible and in most cases dreaded the execution of those dreams. Until I met my husband, Shane. Shane has encouraged me, supported me and often times drug me out to the start line, even when I was most reluctant. Thank you, Shane for not only being my greatest support but also my best friend! You make me a better dreamer because I don't fear the starting line as much with you by my side!

Thank you to my father for always supporting my voice. For giving me a chance to learn to sing and fall in love with music in a way that I never would have without you. Thank you for always encouraging me to bring a uniqueness to my sound and to never fear standing out for that uniqueness.

Thank you to my mother for always being my best friend. Thank you for not only looking at me as your daughter but also a sister in the Lord and friend. Thank you for valuing the Holy Spirit in my life and never letting me settle for anything less than His thoughts about me.

To my children: may you never be limited by glass ceilings or fear. You are the greatest gift from God straight to my heart. Not one moment of your life will be wasted, so run your race unrestrained. I love you with every ounce of me! You are my greatest legacy!

To Josiane: you are far more courageous than you feel at this moment. May your journey give generations to come hope and faith to believe for the impossible. I'm so proud of you!

Dedication

I write this story for the "one."

For the unseen.

For the women kneeling in the dirt, ready to be stoned to death for her crimes. Knowing she is guilty and hearing those lasting, freeing words: "Let him who is without sin among you be the first to throw a stone at her" (John 8:7 ESV).

This is for the single parents daring to take on the role of both for the sake of the one.

This is for the lost one, abandoned and wandering, wondering if "home" is even an option for them anymore.

This story is for all of us. We all lose our way; we all have questions we wish we never did. We all need to be real and vulnerable with the world. This story is for all and yet just for me.

Freedom is found just beyond the horizon of honesty. This is my freedom cry, my last hurrah to the chains and any lasting shackles from my past. I've been a captive for far too long.

May this book bring freedom from the lies, break the chains, and set your heart free to be the person exactly who you were created to be! No regrets, just redemption!

I am here to say, "too far" are words that don't exist in the kingdom where I live, and if no one has told you yet, "it's time to come home!" You carry something beautiful and unique that only you can express! It's been said before: "The world needs who you were created to be," and I'm here to echo that! Not only does the world need who you were created to be, but generations will be impacted and marvel at your life. If only you will just believe in the deep, beautiful purpose for which you have been created!

This story is for you!

Contents

Introduction

The teachers of the law and the Pharisees brought in a woman caught in adultery. They made her stand before the group and said to Jesus, "Teacher, this woman was caught in the act of adultery. In the Law Moses commanded us to stone such women. Now what do you say?" They were using this question as a trap, in order to have a basis for accusing him.

But Jesus bent down and started to write on the ground with his finger. When they kept on questioning him, he straightened up and said to them, "Let any one of you who is without sin be the first to throw a stone at her." Again he stooped down and wrote on the ground.

At this, those who heard began to go away one at a time, the older ones first, until only Jesus was left, with the woman still standing there. Jesus straightened up and asked her, "Woman, where are they? Has no one condemned you?"

"No one, sir," she said.

"Then neither do I condemn you," Jesus declared. "Go now and leave your life of sin."

—John 8:3–11 NIV

As I look at this scripture today, I must admit this scripture rings truer to me than I could ever have imagined. I, too, have been like the women thrown at Jesus's feet, my crimes laid out for all to see.

The dread to look up from the dirt, to look my Savior in the eyes. So much guilt, so much shame. Much like He wrote in the sand for the women thrown at His feet, my mind wonders, "What could He possibly have written about me as I lay there lost in so much sin?"

Slowly everyone has walked away, and now it's just Him and me. It almost seems worse; I can't avoid the inevitable. I glance up, and His eyes meet mine. Instead of anger in His eyes, I am met with compassion and love. Everything inside of me wants to run, yet everything inside of me wants my innocence restored so that I can be with Him, face to face, with nothing between us.

Although I know the woman in John wasn't met with condemnation, I still can't fathom in my own mind how He will respond to me. I should be met with condemnation; I am instead covered in His never-ending love. It confuses me more than I can express. How can He love me so deeply when He knows all that I've done to sin against Him?

Jesus's blood has wiped my slate clean, erased the words of condemnation in my life, and given me a whole new reason for living. I sit and marvel at the life the Lord has delivered me from, and the memories of where I have been seem so far removed from who I am today.

I am reminded of a prophetic word I was given when I was 14 years old: "You will not live the normal goody-two-shoes Christian life!" If I had known then what I know now, perhaps I would have rejected the word. On this side of my prodigal journey, however, I am thankful for the testimony I now have in Him. There is nothing proper or polished about it. My life and my testimony will offend the religious spirit, and I think God knew it. I have a way to commune with the world that I would never have been able to had I not lived the life I have.

We are deeply loved by a Father who kneels with us in our mess. He erases the lies that are truer than we know and calls us

Introduction

His very own. He's not ashamed; He's not annoyed; He isn't embarrassed.

My life went from the woman thrown at his feet in her sin in John 8 to the woman at his feet with her alabaster jar in Matthew 26, pouring her everything out in worship. This is my offering to Him, and I pray it gives every reader hope!

Before diving into my story, I wanted humbly to admit this is my side of my story. There are perspectives that I am acknowledging are my own and probably aren't held by others. I have gone through the long hard process of learning to forgive and let go of the painful things that have happened to me but also to forgive myself for the terrible things I've done to others and myself.

I am not proud of every moment, but I do know that every moment makes me exactly who I am today. I can recall painful moments with my parents and others pointing out lies that were embedded into my heart by the enemy. However, I am in no way angry or still walking in the pain. Although redemption doesn't always mean reconciliation, I can say that I carry no ill feelings for anyone in my past and have released my past as what it is — the past.

1

I Am Done

From the moment I picked up the phone, I could tell something was very off. I was used to the swinging moods. The constant wondering who you may be speaking to, Dr. Jekyll or Mr. Hyde. It was Hyde that caused me the deepest fear, often causing *me* to want to hide. Like an abused dog knows by its master's tone when it is about to be struck, I also had learned to discern when the next blow might strike.

I quickly asked, "What was wrong?" As with most abusive relationships, there is the abuser and the abused. The enabled and the enabler. Often, the abused tries to fix or diffuse the situation, which usually ends up enabling the abuser more than actually fixing anything.

This was the role I had assumed in my life. It wasn't a fact I wanted to admit to myself or to anyone else. I had grown accustomed to covering up and hiding.

He told me in a monotone voice that he had performed a DNA test on our week-old child and today received the results. I immediately filled in the gaps and landed on the conclusion that the test results didn't end up the way he perhaps had hoped.

The last 10 months flashed through my head. How did I end up here? I was honest about sleeping with someone else. I was honest that the father of my unborn baby wasn't clear. It was a scarlet letter that I wore daily.

Ten months earlier...

I remember being terrified to admit that I was weeks late on my period. I couldn't even remember the last time I had a period. I called my ex, Max. I knew he was the last person in the world I should confide in. Even though I knew he wasn't safe, at least I was comfortable in my very scared skin. He already viewed me as filthy and a screw-up; I didn't have to hide my shame from him. Sometimes the only thing that makes rock bottom worse is being there alone, so I welcomed the company, even if it meant more abuse.

We drank a beer as my pregnancy test results were processing. I honestly had no clue how my life could continue if I was pregnant. I had just recently broken up with Max and found myself a brand-new single mother to my one-year-old son. How could I possibly care for him, be pregnant, and work all at the same time? How could I bring a brand-new baby home to this tiny apartment and care for him postpartum and a toddler? And then the result became clear: "positive." My life was over!

It became even more unbearable as Max asked me if the baby was his. I couldn't lie. I wouldn't lie, not to myself or him. The truth was, we hadn't been separated that long and just like my constant track record of jumping from relationship to relationship, often not even done with one relationship before starting the next. I didn't know who's the baby was.

I couldn't imagine it not being Max's because the idea of having two babies with two separate fathers just felt way too unfathomable for me. On the flip side, how could I possibly be having a baby with someone that I'd only known for such a short time and only been dating for a few weeks? Secretly though, I wished it was this new guy's because I knew I couldn't possibly have two children with Max, the person I had vowed never to spend one more second of my life getting hurt and manipulated by.

I was honest, however. I let him know that I had slept with someone else and that I had no clue who's baby I might be carrying. He seemed unphased. It's like he only heard what he wanted to. He may still have an opportunity to get me back. He assured me I was okay and should move back in with our son. No matter the results of who the father was of this new baby, we could be a family once again.

I had some very big decisions to make, and I couldn't carry this burden alone. I needed someone I loved and trusted to speak truth back into my bleeding soul, but I was terrified to tell anyone of my mess. I had to tell at least my family, but they were the very ones I dreaded telling the most.

I remember the night vividly, dropping by my parents' house, knowing I had to be honest about my life. I remember being terrified not only to admit that I was pregnant with my second child but, to add to that, there was such a short time span between the guys I had been dating that I wasn't 100% sure who's the baby even was.

I hated everything about that conversation! I hated the look of shock on my parent's faces. I hated the words that came out of my own mouth. I hated that I "knew" better than all of this, and yet here I stood! I hated the fact that I felt like I should be celebrating the birth of a new baby but instead, inside, a piece of me was dying. I hated that this felt like the most beautiful gift, a life, in the most reckless of circumstances. How had my life become this messy?

My life was reckless, my soul was empty, and I wasn't sure how to hang on for one second longer.

My parents stood close by my side. They helped me with my first son, and they were dedicated to this second baby, no matter who the father was. They were dedicated to me. No matter how much I felt I didn't deserve that, they never hung it over my head. They never made me feel like less of a person or a mother.

In some ways, that was comforting, but in others, it stung even worse! How was I their daughter? How was this the life they had ever dreamed of for their daughter? They certainly didn't raise me like this.

I wanted to hear from them what a disgrace I was. I wanted them to look me in the eye and tell me what a screw-up I was. Grace was almost worse. I knew I didn't deserve grace; I couldn't even beg for mercy.

Hopelessness covered my heart as I entered this second pregnancy.

My parents didn't have space or room for the growing family that I was carrying, and I hated to feel like my poor choices would affect their lives. I moved back in with my abuser, Max, out of fear. I couldn't do this alone, and I still had this very broken idea that children being raised by single parents would be worse off. I broke all promises to myself and did what had to have been right by my boys. I knew it was the worst decision I had ever made, but I also felt I had no option.

I had learned before to live with the abuse; I could learn to do it again. Surely, his promises of not caring who's the new baby would be were true! Surely, when he said he didn't care and we could be a happy family of four, that had to have been true. At least these are the lies that I told myself as I packed up my apartment of freedom and moved back into the shackles that I had just freed myself from.

The truth was he didn't need to say much to convince me. I was desperate! I wanted the perfect life, yet I was the furthest thing from perfection.

Max's controlling grip grew almost as quickly as my stomach did over those months. He had known that I worked with the possible father of my growing child and forbade me to have any contact with him. I would have to go to work early and leave during lunches to avoid any contact with my co-worker. He knew I was pregnant as well and agreed to leave me be until the baby was born, but then he would want a paternity test just like Max did.

I would sit and pray to God by myself as I was falling asleep that magically God would help me to win the lottery. If only I had money, I could take my boys and run. If God would provide me an out, I would take it. I would search my life for a sign that I was worth helping out of this mess.

Even the idea of meeting my newest sweet boy brought me terror. How was I going to raise another child with this man? I didn't love him; I didn't even love myself.

These were the longest 10 months of my life. The night sky seemed empty and bleak as darkness settled deep into my soul.

Soon, I welcomed my second son into the world. I held him closer than the first as I could tell within moments of seeing him that he wasn't Max's. I was a protective mother from the second I knew. I wasn't sure how this all was going to unravel, but I knew that in time it would.

Snap back to Mr. Hyde. Wait! What did you just say? You couldn't raise this bastard child as your own? I snapped back into the moment, and this was my reality. I became defensive within seconds. These results were very probable; none of this should have come as a shock or even a surprise. I could only see from my own perspective the walls of our lives crumbling and knowing in an instant everything would change. I had to think for my son in that moment, though. I couldn't allow my allegiance to stand with a man that had been very emotionally and mentally abusive for years.

My self-made tower began to crumble. I struggled to formulate a clear way out. After all, this was my mess, this was my life, and I had made all the choices that landed me in this very moment. Except now, as another relationship crumbled, it wasn't just me left in the balance. I had two innocent, beautiful boys.

I could no longer be selfish. I didn't care. I had to do what was right for my kids. It didn't matter what the solution was going to look like. I had made a promise to myself that my boys wouldn't feel the effects of my sin. My sin and shame weren't theirs to carry, and I certainly wasn't going to allow that to be their destiny. They didn't choose this life. I wasn't going to let this precious new baby grow up ever believing he was any less than his brother because of my choices.

I stared into the eyes of my two little boys. It was in that moment that a strength rose from within me. Perhaps all my prayers for the lottery didn't come true, but God was still faithful to bring about an amount of courage and bravery that would lead the boys and me into a new life. His promises and love for me never failed, even though I strayed so far from home. Could it be that perhaps even despite my mess, God could still have some sort of plan for my life? Maybe even a second chance?

Alone in the dark of my lonely room, I made my final declaration: "I am done!" I remember whispering it at first, like even I couldn't even believe I was saying it. As I felt the strength become stronger, I was able to say it louder and clearer.

"I am done!"

2

Hope Found in a Rock

I was raised in a simple time. I was born in northern California to two young parents. Our family of four managed our simple life with relative ease. It was just my older brother and me.

My mom worked part-time from home as a professional seamstress, which meant I was always very close to her. She was very gentle and kind. She loved creating and teaching us to be creative as well. Everything my mom touched looked like a masterpiece to me. I was always happy to try and catch her creativity, even if I wasn't ever able to do as well as her. She loved Jesus very much and truly made it her number one goal to raise my brother and me with as much as that love for Jesus as she could. She didn't waste much time pouring her vast amount of love and wisdom into me. She didn't dumb God down for me. Instead, she shared deep truths and revelation as if I were old enough to comprehend and understand. Much of the wisdom and insight went over my head, but my heart captured it all.

I remember being very young and having a much different relationship and understanding of God than the other kids my age. I wasn't just reading Bible stories and coloring color sheets; I was listening to prophetic words and dreams. My life was marked by the prophet Bob Jones's cassette teaching of an interaction he had with heaven where Jesus asked him, "Did you learn to love?" I never really dabbled in the shallow end of my faith; it felt deep all around me from the beginning.

These were among the many truths my mom taught me at a very young age. God wasn't distant but close, and through the Holy Spirit, we could learn so much more about him. Faith wasn't in the four walls of the church but in the person of Jesus. You put your faith in Jesus, not necessarily the people of the church, not hating the church by any means but certainly not getting lost in that being your only outlet to God.

I didn't feel elite; rather, I felt I developed a way to talk and communicate about and to God as if it didn't rely on someone or something else to do it for me.

Now, I experienced my dad through a lens of fear. He had big dark eyebrows and a huge mustache that hid any smile that may have been underneath. He wasn't a mean man but also hadn't learned much about how to be a father from his father. So at the ripe age of 21, when I was born, it was like out of the frying pan and into the fire.

Both of my parents came from homes where communication consisted of two extremes: yelling and dictatorship or silence. Support and affirmation were unheard of, and both my parents set out to make a life for themselves a little differently than they had both experienced themselves.

Despite not being given many tools from his own family, my dad was always trying to grow and pivot.

I remember clearly when I was six years old, he asked me why I was so afraid of him. I only had so many words, but I remember telling him that when he raised his voice at me, it scared me. From that moment on, my father never raised his voice at me again. I learned the things people are willing to do to show their love for another.

Growing up, I felt like I was an average girl. I didn't require anything special, but I did want to know I was special. This was something I struggled with deeply. (Words were something my father didn't have many of, and encouraging words seemed even more scarce.)

Faith was something that almost came easily to me. I never struggled to believe anything I heard about God until I started developing what I would now call anxiety when I was around eight years old.

As the sun would begin to set, this sense of panic would grip my being. I couldn't describe what I was experiencing, but all of me felt panicked. Because I couldn't describe what I was experiencing, it made it very difficult to get help for what was going on.

I would frantically pace my room before bed and often fell asleep late into the night just to reawaken and go crawl into bed with my parents or on my brother's floor. Somehow the presence of someone else caused me peace. I could escape this fear as if their presence would protect me from it.

I would spend the hours I was at school forgetting about my fear the night before. By the time school had ended, I was already becoming nervous about how the evening and night would go.

I had nothing logical to blame my fear on. Neither I nor my parents had any grid for spiritual warfare. So I would lay awake at night in dread.

About three months into this dreadful season, I can recall my mom taking my brother and me to the beach for a painting day. This was a special event as we had both been given painting supplies for Christmas, and my mom was going to take us to the beach to break them in.

I loved the beach. The sand, the crisp air, the freedom. Nothing holding you back or in, just liquid freedom as far as the eye could carry you.

That day, I stood at the water's edge and decided I was going to have it out with God. I was done with all this nighttime nonsense. I couldn't handle this anymore. While most of my friends were enjoying their third-grade lives, I was busy wondering why God was torturing me with mine. It's not like I was afraid of anything; I just had this unexplainable fear that would come over me. It caused me to panic and become afraid to be alone, even though I knew in my heart I had nothing to be afraid of. Not being able to tie it to anything rational just fed into the mounting distress, "Would this always be my life?"

So, there I stood, and I yelled out in my head, "God, if you're really real, I need to see you! If you are all the things that I've heard of, this 'faith' thing isn't working. I need to see with my own eyes—your love for me! If you are real, I need to know!"

I'd love to say the clouds parted, and there before me on the water stood Jesus himself. Instead of hearing His voice, I heard the soothing sound of the waves and seagulls. As I turned away from the water to head back to my painting, I saw a rock on the beach that caught my eye. Something inside of me knew I had to pick it up and turn it over. Upon turning it over, there carved out of the center of the rock was the shape of a perfect heart. My eyes filled with tears, and like a blanket, the love of God covered my little heart. I knew from that moment on, without a shadow of a doubt, that God was real. He wasn't afraid of my questions and doubts. He wasn't distant and far off. He was willing to give me a "sign" rather than condemn my lack of faith.

Much like the story of Nathanael meeting Jesus for the first time in the Bible. "'How do you know me?' Nathanael asked. Jesus answered, 'I saw you while you were still under the fig tree before Philip called you'" (John 1:48 NIV). It was the fact that Jesus "saw" him that changed Nathanael's whole world. All I needed to know was that I was seen, and for my young heart, God chose a heart in a rock to represent his love and to show me that He saw me.

That heart represented everything I needed to carry on even if the battle inside didn't go away. That rock represented breakthrough, a weapon. My anxiety stood like a giant in my life. Much like David was given a rock to defeat Goliath, this was the weapon God had given me to defeat my giant. It was his love—his perfect love—that would see this fear and anxiety meet its match and eventually find its ending in my life.

I clung to that rock with everything inside of my being. As much as I would have loved for darkness not to enter my mind at night and to have found instant relief, it was the first blow to the giant of fear and anxiety in my life. The walls of fear were beginning to crack, and through the cracks I could see light shining through. That light was enough hope to press into God to see this thing break completely in my life.

One night, as that familiar feeling was beginning to surface again, I sat with my mom, and she began to give me some scriptures to cling to and wage war with. She knew my struggles and was always trying to help me find a way to resolve them. The first one was 1 John 4:18, which states, "There is no fear in love. But perfect love drives out fear." The second was 1 Thessalonians 5:16–18, which reads, "Rejoice always, pray continually, give thanks in all circumstances." My mom suggested that I start a "thankfulness journal." I could include everything from the meal I had the night before to the deepest elements of my life. So that when fear began to creep in, I would pull it out and start reciting the very truths that I knew were real and true. I became so accustomed to this list I practically had it memorized.

I found myself becoming the true me as I would read and recite this list. I wasn't lost in worry or fear. I wasn't consumed with gloom. I was bubbly and thankful. I found my smile again, and in the midst of a dark season, the very foundation of who I was created to be was being laid. I may not have known it in the moment, but everything was being set; everything was changed as I learned to weather the storms of life through thanksgiving and praise.

3

God Uses Shame

Time passed much as it always does. In time, the terror of my night season was dissipating as I was experiencing some freedom.

My family had moved to Oregon, and we were starting over. My mother's sister had been living in Oregon for a few years after the passing of my grandmother. California was quickly growing, and the cost of living was becoming unbearable for our little family. The final straw was when our landlords decided to sell the house we were renting. It was time to move north where we could save to buy our own home. We had a new home in Oregon—new friends, new schools, and a new community. Life was still fairly simple as most days consisted of school and play with the weekly Sunday service and home groups that my parents were part of.

I was in sixth grade and just beginning to notice the areas of my life that were different than others. Whether it was how much money we had and how that related to the clothes that the other kids could afford that we couldn't or the way certain girls' hair was styled just so. I began to compare how they looked and presented their outward beauty to who I was and very quickly began to question myself. Without a strong affirming voice from my father, all I could conclude was that something was off with me.

I wasn't able to see the value in me and my heart without tripping over how my looks did or didn't capture that. I remember one afternoon at school, a boy told me I had a big butt. This was the first time I ever even thought about my body in a big or small way. I had always just thought of myself as me, and the skin I was in was just part of that.

I couldn't just blow off what he said. That fiery arrow that was aimed straight for my heart hit its target and sunk in deeply. It not only made me question how I felt about myself, but it also made me begin to question why God didn't make me more like some of the other girls that I so looked up to.

I spent the rest of my sixth-grade year tying a sweatshirt around my waist so that no one could see my backside. Where was Sir Mix-a-Lot when I needed him? I don't know why that one tiny comment—that lie—consumed me. I certainly knew I wasn't the prettiest girl around, but the idea that others were noticing that enforced the lie that something was, in fact, wrong with me. It wouldn't be until much later in life that I realized the battle for my identity and the confusion that I felt over beauty was waged in my life at a very young age. This is where the lie began to take root.

So much was shifting and taking place in my life that year. I also began to play in the school band and sing in their choir.

I knew I had always loved music, but I also loved that it was a point of connection between my dad and me, something that was challenging to find. I found that playing music or singing were the languages that my dad and I could speak the best with one another.

I had always known that music was the way to my dad's heart. I had grown up watching him play guitar in bands and leading worship. Every Saturday morning the music would be cranked up, and his guitar would be on. For as long as I can remember, I don't recall a time that my dad wasn't playing his guitar. He would sneak me into the city for dates to listen to music long after my bedtime when his guitar teacher was playing. He would sit and talk to me all about music, his favorite artists, style, and genres. I didn't understand most of it, but I would sit and listen, fully engaged because this was the place where my dad would fully engage with me. I tried sports, and that didn't work. I tried other things, but nothing created for us what music did.

Where starting and having a conversation with my dad was very hard, it had become less of a struggle now that I was also a "musician." I think it created a connection point for him, but what I found was it was something that I was praised for doing and a common ground with my dad.

Returning to my desk after a parent-teacher conference, I saw a tiny yellow note hidden inside my pencil box. It read, "Seems you are doing great in school. I am so happy you are doing music! I love you so much! Dad" This was the first love note I had ever received from my dad. I sat at my desk as tears streamed down my face. I wanted to hide my emotion in that moment as it seemed so silly. Perhaps to the other kids, it would seem so small and insignificant. Not to me, though; this meant the world to me.

This wasn't only the first time my dad left me a little note. It may have been one of the first times that he told me I was good at something and that he was proud of me. It was like a hidden oasis in the desert that was my life with my dad. I had no idea how starved I was for affirmation until I got some.

I was determined not only to keep doing music but to do it to my greatest abilities. If this was what would happen from just joining band and choir, I could only begin to imagine if I really "made" something of myself in music.

Not only did I realize that my love for music gained me connection with my dad, but I realized it opened a whole new way to express my praise and gratitude to God. I realized that what I learned years prior in my "thankfulness journal" was worship. Coming to God with my praise and thanksgiving was ushering me right into His throne room. God had been forming and fashioning my heart even through my pain to do one of the main things I was created for: worship!

What if, in the darkness, God was actually doing the very thing He promised? What if He was turning the very thing that the enemy planned for evil for my good? What if the enemy's plan to steal my peace, joy, sanity, and connection to God was the very thing that would connect me to Him the most?

With this new revelation of the connection that music created with both my earthly and heavenly Father and my own deep passion for music, I ran after music with everything inside of me.

I sang in choirs, I played flute in band, and I learned to play piano, but nothing brought me to life quite like singing on my own. I would listen to Amy Grant for hours upon hours. Music was the one constant in my life. I would wear tapes out from listening to them over and over again. I found I could listen to a song, and after one listen, I had almost memorized the lyrics and melody. I wouldn't say I was a "natural" because other than how my memory aided in the learning process, every step of the way was work. I was never the best, but I was also never ashamed of working hard at the thing that I loved so deeply.

I never really dreamed of finding fame as a singer. I just knew I had to be singing. It was the one thing that I knew I could do; it was the one thing that brought me fully to life.

Time passed, and my abilities as a musician grew. My dad had pulled me in on the worship team, and I was running after Jesus now more than ever. I was heavily involved in youth group, the worship team, and in my off time, my dad and I and some guys from the worship team formed a band. It wasn't worship, and it wasn't full-on secular.

We spent hours practicing, and much of who I was dreaming of becoming was being molded in the hands of this band. I had no idea where it might head, but I knew that I could see myself running in this direction for the rest of my life.

God Uses Shame

Much to my amazement, we were invited to play our first show ever, TOMfest, in Stevenson, Washington. TOMfest was a Christian music festival. This was the day we had all been practicing for all these hours.

This was the first time I had ever thought about music as a performance, like I needed to figure out who I would be as a performer, not just a musician. I went to the mall and picked out a pair of tight black bell-bottom polyester pants with big green flowers on the bottom, a stripped white Adidas type top, platform shoes, and to top it off, I bought some silver lipstick. (I'm pretty sure the silver lipstick was my dad's idea.)

I had created the look to go with the trendy 90s sound that I had truly begun to master. I sounded much like a mixture between Poe, Alanis Morissette, and Mazzy Star, and now I also had my very own look to go with it.

I typically sang backup and harmonized, but this festival would not only be the first time I sang in front of a crowd that I wasn't leading in worship but also that I was leading a song.

As we set up and sound-checked, I remember quickly noting that there weren't enough speaker monitors for our rather large band. It didn't seem like a big deal at the time, but little did I know that this would end up being a tragedy.

As the first song ended, I was up! I knew every part of this song; I practically could have sung it backward. This was it— every daydream I had ever had about performing was coming true. Maybe I never dreamed much of the stage, but now I could see it coming into plain sight. *This* is what I was made for.

The song ended, and then the last songs of the set. I was on a whole other planet; it was everything I hoped it would be and more. Although it was over in a whirlwind, we hung around to hear a few bands before making the long drive home.

As soon as we arrived home, our friend that had recorded the whole thing put the VHS in, and we were all excited to watch how we all looked and sounded. I remember lying on the floor, taking in every bit of our performance. It was almost surreal.

Sure, the quality of sound and sight wasn't great, but I could see this heading somewhere incredible.

As my solo song began, I remember nervously watching with one eye open. The first verse was a little rocky, but overall, I was becoming more comfortable with the direction things were heading until the chorus hit and everything about my dreams of singing crumbled. As I mentioned before, I couldn't hear myself at all, so everything I was singing was just based upon muscle memory of maybe where the melody lay in the song.

It was like a bad accident; I just couldn't seem to look away. I was literally singing the song in a whole other key than the rest of the band. I am quite certain that if you muted the band, you could have heard me singing it perfectly in this other key, just happened to be different than everyone else around me.

I was mortified. I was so embarrassed, I could barely stand to watch it myself, much less with everyone else in that room. Friends, family, and band members were laughing and cringing. I had never wanted to crawl into a hole and die more than I wanted to in that moment.

I ran to my room and slammed the door behind me. How could this be happening? I had worked so, so hard. This had been the one thing that I felt I was actually good at. This was supposed to be the safety in my life, the connection point to God my Father. How in the world could He have allowed me to fail so terribly? Bitter hot tears streamed down my face as I was disgusted with God and then with myself. I tore off the outfit that only hours prior had been my joy, now something I vowed never to wear again!

That wouldn't be the only vow that I made that night. I also vowed that I would never, ever put myself in that position to be humiliated like that. I would never sing again!

I sat in a dazed stupor. Everything was spinning, and nothing was making sense. I wanted a place to land, but even the ground seemed like the furthest thing from my feet.

God Uses Shame

I went to my mom to try and regain some perspective; she knew of all my hard work leading up to that day. She had seen me fail so miserably. More than that, though, she had always been my sounding board through thick and thin. It had been some distant years between the two of us, but I knew I could trust her with my disillusionment and confusion. I opened up about my anger toward God and my humiliation over the whole thing. How could God have let something so embarrassing happen? Why wouldn't He shelter me from the pain that was being caused by my humiliation? Music had been my safe place, and what I seemed to know of God at the time, I felt He should have protected that safe place. My mom sat and listened as I angrily recalled the whole day's events and my deep fear of ever singing again.

In that moment, she said the only thing her current filter gave her insight to. You see, she had witnessed me becoming more and more outwardly confident and excited about the festival. She had also seen me doing things to add to the performance, whether it be clothes or make-up. Our lens in which we saw God left no room for such things. "Well, honey, you were getting pretty prideful!" She smiled and hugged me, hoping that comfort was found in knowing the "why" behind the mess I was experiencing.

Prideful? I didn't even know how to be prideful! If anything, this was the first time I had ever been confident in anything that I was doing. How could it have been that confidence and pride could so easily be interchangeable? For some reason, confidence equaled pride at the church we were attending, and we all know what God allowed, if not caused, if we were prideful. I was walking out my "fall" for all the world to see.

If my pain level was a seven before these very simple words, it now had escalated to a 10! What I heard her say was, "If I ever become prideful, God will humiliate me to deal with that pride!" The very thing I should have taken *to* the Lord was the very thing leading me away from Him. It was in this moment that a lie was planted in the garden of my heart: "God uses shame!" When we step outside of his grace or will, instead of bringing loving correction or even discipline, He will use shame to bring us back into order.

4

The Cost of Love

I slowly began to spiral again, although the dread from my previous dark season didn't scare me anymore. Secretly, I began to crave its familiar touch. I was beginning to feel like the depths of me were becoming fractured. One part desperately wanted my relationship with Jesus to grow. The other part was so starved for love, attention, and to be seen, I would have done just about anything to get those needs met.

It was a tough season at home. Both my parents were busy with ministry. My mom served as a prophetic teacher at our church, and my dad was the worship leader, but both were on the leadership team for the church. They both were working and just living a basic life. I was busy trying to figure out who I was and didn't have too much truth being spoken amidst the lies that were so readily available inside my own head.

I didn't stop singing, as much as I wanted to after my utter failure at TOMFest. I did, however, adopt a fear of ever gaining confidence in myself again as it may be viewed as pride by others and, even worse, by God. I knew what would happen if He thought I was becoming confident or prideful.

Singing was different now, though, tainted by insecurity and fear of failure. I was terrified to sing out and even more paranoid that I was singing out of key.

So, I tried to spend my days like most teens, days full of school and concentrating on my studies and friends. But my evenings were filled with church events and band practice. On the outside, everything was clicking, but deep inside me, this gaping hole was growing.

I had developed a healthy dose of self-hatred that I wasn't able to shake no matter how hard I tried. It started with an annoying feeling that would come over me; I just felt out of place and unknown by my parents, by God, and by myself. Slowly, in time, what had started as an annoying feeling or lie grew into an all-consuming feeling.

Because so much of my time was spent with youth group, most of my friends were youth group friends. Our ages ranged from middle school to college-age and everything in between. As most young girls do, I had an eye for all the cute boys, but it seemed that none of them quite had the same eye for me. This could have been a blessing in disguise, but I didn't feel that way at the time. What probably saved me many pointless heart attachments that would have ended just felt like further unworthiness and rejection.

I tried everything I could think of to fit in with the boys in youth group. Up until then, I was typically the goofy, light-hearted girl in the group. I was known for my laughter and smile, then my depth and typical teen moodiness. The only way I knew how to interact with the opposite sex was how I interacted with my older brother. So, lots of teasing, hitting, and stealing various hats and other random items. Pretty much, I was your annoying little sister, but really, I thought you were cute. All you might want to do was to go flirt with the more mature girls. Instead, you were being distracted with the likes of me as I desperately threw another punch your way in hopes of gaining your affection.

I had no clue who I was, how I was coming across, and why all the other girls seemed to get the attention I so craved.

One of my best friends happened to be one of "those" girls who didn't have any problem getting the guys' attention. If anything, I couldn't believe how much it seemed that every single guy was just waiting to shamelessly be flirted with and flirt with her.

I couldn't understand it. She wasn't silly and giggly and full of life. She was moody and pouted when she didn't get what she wanted from the boys. It seemed so counter-intuitive to what one might be after, but it was working, and that was intriguing to me.

Where my attempts at gaining attention, approval, and validation weren't working, hers were. Where I was failing at treating boys like brothers, she was flirting like a real-life teenage girl, and the boys were lining up one right after the other. I would make myself available as she would act withdrawn, dark, and hard to get. The preverbal lightbulb went off, and I knew I had to switch my game up a bit. My goal was no longer innocent and cute, playful, and fun; it was going to be pouty and flirtatious, moody, and hard to get.

You see, to me, it seemed simple, I was lacking what she had, and if I could gain attention and validation by flirting or at least flirting like she did, I'd do it! I felt I couldn't capture the attention of my father at home. So, I figured I would fill this hole inside me with another male's attention.

If flirting gained attention, and attention equaled desire, then desire must equal worthiness. At the end of the day, that is what my heart was searching for: worthiness. Worthy of time, worthy of attention, worthy of love.

If all I learned from that friendship was the power of proper flirting, it might have only been a slight setback in my life. But I also learned a very dark secret. If one doesn't eat, one will become skinny. And if one is skinny, one will also do better with the boys. So desperate to find a solution, I created a formula from my friend's life. I saw the way the boys craved attention from her, so I boiled it down to two things: her flirting and her looks. No one ever said that she was desirable because she was thin. I just needed something to strive for.

I had never really thought of myself as fat, but I also hadn't ever thought of myself as pretty either. There was an obvious disconnect between boys and me, and I was bound to connect what that might be.

I had decided that this driving thought at the back of my mind—this idea that I had a big butt, that boys didn't like me, that I couldn't get my father's attention and verbal praise—*all* of this just *must* come from the fact that I was fat and ugly!

I know what you're thinking: that seems absurd, but let me tell you what, you don't know until you know! Being starved for love and attention causes you to draw conclusions that no sane, high-identity person would ever draw.

So, day after day, I slowly began the long, hard process of training myself to hate my body and to despise food even more because it was the thing that made my body fat!

At first, you really couldn't notice that much. It was the 90s, and grunge was still in! I was lost in pants that were my brother's and baby doll dresses and huge purple Doc Martens. No one could really tell what my body looked like underneath the baggy clothes, and our family dinners were totally nonexistent as ministry became a full-time baby for my parents. They weren't around in the morning for breakfast, and they weren't there to see if I packed a lunch. Honestly, it was easy to get away with. Most days, I would bring 50 cents to school to buy a Fudgsicle, which was 45 calories, and I remember it would be the thing that would carry me through my days at school.

Slowly, my body began to change over time, and my friend at youth group began to notice. She decided to help me get into some clothes that were my own size. I remember her telling me that no guy was ever going to want to date me if I was still wearing my brother's pants. For Christmas, she purchased me my first pair of Levi's, in my own size, along with a couple of cuter, more feminine tops.

So, although the tighter clothes started to gain me some attention at school and in youth group from the guys, it also gained me some much-needed attention from my father. I remember him being so concerned, almost yelling at me for not eating. He threatened even to go to school and watch me eat my lunch, to be with me while I was making my lunch, to make sure that I was packing healthy food. Now, perhaps for a normal teenager, that seems like the most embarrassing threat ever, but not to me. This seemed like hope! What if my dad actually did come and eat lunch with me at school? I was in high school; that idea should be the furthest thing from my mind. But to me, it said, "Sarah, you are worth me spending time with. You are worth me coming to your school and giving up what I want to do to make sure you are cared for."

No one ever said it was healthy, but this was the climate of my barely beating heart. Much as a toddler might throw a fit to gain their parents' attention, I would starve myself for as long as it took to get the time and attention I so deeply needed.

The threats were just that, though: threats. My dad never came to my school to have lunch with me. He never stood beside me in the kitchen to make sure I was packing a lunch. I had no idea how to tell him how desperate I had become, and I think he thought he was doing what he needed to do as a father. After all, his only example was his own dad. Yelling and verbal abuse. Drunkenness and total narcissism were the examples he had to go off. My dad was treated completely differently from his two sisters and never seemed to measure up in his father's eyes compared to them. So, compared to his father, my father was leaps and bounds further ahead.

In walked my first boyfriend. Oh man, all this hard work of learning to flirt and starving myself was paying off! He was one of the older kids that had joined the youth group my freshman year. I had finally earned the attention I was after. Not only was this boy cute, he was quite a bit older, but also a lot of the other girls liked him—specifically, my one girlfriend who taught me all the flirting tricks. Not even she could turn his head, but I, on the other hand, was the one he was interested in.

I had never felt this way before. It was like everything I had hoped it would be and then some. He was just as broken and confused about life as I was. He was a musician and loved Jesus, and I was convinced my only aim in life was to finish school so I could marry him. I felt seen for the first time in a very long time.

I didn't have huge goals or aspirations beyond music for my life. In fact, before music was even in my life, the main thing I had always desired was to get married early and become a mom. When others were sharing their dreams of becoming doctors and teachers, I was daydreaming and naming my unborn children. This hope and dream seemed to be something so far off before, but now it was coming into full focus.

God had finally heard my prayers. He had answered the cries of my lonely heart with someone who would have done anything for me.

It was a whirlwind of young love. We weren't really allowed to date for two reasons, really. The first was because I couldn't date until I was 16. Secondly, he was five years older than me! Not a big deal when you are 20 and 25, but when I was 15 and he was 20, it proved to be way too much of a gap for my parents, perhaps even the law!

We spent the better part of a year flirting and sneaking around behind my parents' back with this secret love affair. It tore me up inside that I was having to choose between this boy who really met my needs of being seen and my parents' wishes and trust. I wasn't one to lie. I hated the way it ate me up inside, but as I saw it, I had no choice. I had gone too many years being overlooked, feeling not special and totally ignored. It was my season to finally be something in my own eyes. I wasn't powerful enough of a person to express any of this. So instead, I did the only thing I could think of: lie! Lie to my parents about my pain, lie to my parents about finding love, and retreat in this boy's arms. It felt like too big of a mountain to climb to open up and be vulnerable with my parents, so I kept my heart and life hidden.

One of the best parts about this relationship was that I didn't have to be that moody, pouty teen that I thought I would have to be. I got to be my goofy self. Being funny was my thing. I loved to make other people laugh, but more than anything, I loved to make myself laugh. Despite this deep ache growing inside, I was pretty joyful.

Until one day when that all changed! My friends in youth group saw the path I was headed down. They knew my parents asked me not to pursue this man as a boyfriend. They knew I was lying, so they went to my parents and told them.

I will never forget pacing the floor in my bedroom when they sent me off to my room after telling me that I wouldn't be seeing or talking to him ever again. How could this be happening? I had already planned my whole life with this person, and now I was never going to see him again! How could we still all go to the same church? Were they just going to ask him to leave the church? It became clear that I hadn't honored my parents' wishes, but it also was made clear that he wasn't interested in honoring my parents' wishes either. Something, had they decided to take up with the law, would have ended very badly for him. How was I even going to live without him? I contemplated jumping out of my window and walking to a payphone having him pick me up, and I would be the one to tell my parents how this was going to go down, or I wasn't going to be living with them anymore.

I couldn't do it, though. I didn't want to end the relationship with my family. I didn't want to break our family apart. I just wanted to be wanted; I wanted to have a relationship in which I felt wanted and had my parents. That wasn't going to happen, though, and so I chose where God led me to stay: with my parents. I didn't have a real chance to say goodbye to him. We were torn apart due to our lies and the betrayal of my parents' trust. I used a friend in my life to give him the message that I would wait, no matter the length of time, and he would do the same for me.

What started as an ache inside of me had now grown beyond a pain that I could ignore. I dove face-first into God and other friendships around me. God was faithful to provide other friendships and distractions from the pain I was running from on the inside.

My parents began to regain trust, and I was proving to be trustworthy now that the distraction of boys wasn't in the picture. I think a piece of me was still holding on to hope that once I turned 16, I could date, and my first love would still be waiting for me, and my parents might give us a chance to fix what we had broken.

Well, time passed as it always does, and I found myself on my 16th birthday even more lost and confused than the year prior. I should have been rejoicing. I had worked hard to rebuild trust with my parents. So technically, dating was finally on the table for me, and this relationship that I would have given up everything for a year prior was now on my doorstep. Yet, I didn't find myself wanting to open the door. My feelings had changed. I wasn't in the same place as I was the year prior. I didn't want to run off with this boy I had once loved because I had found another boy who caught my attention.

Teens are fickle and, honestly, should never be given the power to make such choices, but it's in those moments of choice that history is established. We all have to learn to make decisions and suffer the consequences, one way or the other.

I hid my face in my father's loving embrace, and I sobbed into his chest on my 16th birthday. I know I had vowed to wait for this boy forever, but now, I couldn't handle the idea of dating him. We hadn't made an official plan to date when I was 16, but he did start coming around some church services more again, and my parents began trusting us to perhaps date when I was 16. "I just don't think I love him anymore, daddy! I don't want to date him, and I'm afraid to tell him that." It was probably the most compassionate I had experienced my father up until that point. He held me, then wiped my tears away as he told me it was going to be okay. I am sure something deep inside of him was finding comfort in knowing that his baby girl was no longer interested in dating a 21-year-old man. The one stumbling block in our relationship was being removed, and much to my surprise, it was bringing me closer to my dad.

I had never experienced this type of relief in his arms. I had never imagined that letting go of the thing I thought was sustaining me would bring me to the one thing I wanted. This moment could have lasted forever, and I would have been okay with that. I didn't need a boy. If I could just have this man, my father, I would have been content.

My dad stayed close and connected to me for a couple of days. I remember feeling like I really had his attention, and he was genuinely concerned for the condition of my heart. He would pull me in to do things with him that perhaps he wouldn't have done before. We celebrated my birthday in the most grandiose of ways with my whole family and friends. I really had hope that things were beginning to shift in my life. Sadly, it didn't last long, and before too long, life took over, busyness won, and I was lost in the shuffle of life again.

As I was saying goodbye to one crush, another one had emerged. This time this boy was nothing like me. He was another older boy from youth group. His personality was dark and mysterious. He wasn't readily available, required pursuit, and played the game of hard-to-get way far beyond my level. He was a musician as well, and we had played worship together and then also in our band together. He had always been dating and then engaged to a friend and another band member. And although I wasn't dating, my heart was always spoken for. We had been in youth group together for quite some time, and truth be told, he wasn't exactly a kind person. He had a short temper and would often cut down my goofy personality as it was just too bubbly for the likes of a poetry-reading, Pearl Jam fanatic, morbid person like himself.

I don't know where or even why I became interested in him. Maybe it was this lack calling deep from within; maybe it's because in the middle of my mess, he stepped in and told me he had left his fiancée because he had feelings for me. I don't really know where it started, but I remember being shocked that this guy was telling me he had fallen for me.

"You better not be messing with my head!" was my response when he told me he had feelings for me one night after band practice. I remember sitting in my living room after my parents had gone to bed. We were two friends and bandmates hanging out. I may have had a slight crush on him at times, but there were no signs that this admission of feelings was coming. This guy was known for his mind games, and everyone around him had been sucked in a least a time or two. I wasn't his "type," and he must have known that just as much as I did. Here he was, though, confessing his feelings. I was lacking. I would be lying if I hadn't had some sort of crush at some point. These were the things fairytales were made from, right? Things were going to make a shift for the better if this popular guy was going to fall for me. To break off his engagement because of a crush he had on me, surely, I must be carrying some sort of value deep inside that even I hadn't discovered yet.

It wasn't long before I had changed everything about my light, bubbly personality to match his. Laughing didn't seem like it was attractive; being mysterious and withdrawn were. A smile might show weakness, and so a scowl was where strength was found. Everything about my normal personality had to be shifted to match his in order to date him. I learned a hard lesson in that relationship. I was like a chameleon; I could change myself based on who I was dating in order to receive the love that I needed. I may never have learned how to do it with my dad, but I was learning how to do it in this relationship, and it was working.

Time quickly passed as I was deeply immersed in this relationship. It wasn't a happy relationship; it was often still filled with mind games and violent mood swings. Instead of expressing his fears and emotions, he would come up with elaborate lies to push and pull me away, whichever suited his desires better at the time. He would make up lies about far-off relationships, laced water with drugs in it, and people dying. I had never experienced such mind games, so I happened to fall for them every time. The moment of vulnerability that was shown when he confessed his feelings to me was long gone, and I quickly realized vulnerability was something that would never happen again.

His walls were up, and it quickly became clear that my role in the relationship was to learn how to clear those walls. Short of those brief moments of feeling chosen and set apart in the beginning of our relationship, value and affirmation weren't things that were offered in this relationship. I wasn't just dating my dad; I was dating the mean, mind-game version of my dad. Not only was I not given any value, other than the value of chasing him down, but I also had to learn how to deal with someone's anger. The smallest things would set him off. Without any warning, we could be enjoying our day, and the wrong song would come on the radio, the wrong glance from a stranger across the room. There was no rhyme or reason to what might trigger his anger, so I never knew what might make him angry next. My dad may have been a lot of things, but angry wasn't one of them. He may not have known how to build me up but tearing me down was never his goal. Yet here I found myself in the arms of a man that was everything I hated about my life and then some.

Even despite my fear of failure, music seemed to be the only thing holding me afloat. I wasn't singing songs of praise and thanksgiving any longer, though. Alice in Chains, Smashing Pumpkins, and Pearl Jam were my new top favorites as that's what was best-loved by those around me.

In this difficult season, God blessed me with a wonderful friend. She was my parents' age and had a son a couple of years older than me, but she was like the older sister I never had. Her name was Peggi, and I adored her and delighted in her adoring me as well. She saw past my dark superficial mask and knew I had always been light, and she was determined that I knew my worth. She would blare Michael W. Smith, Margret Becker, and Nicole Nordman in the car as she taught me to drive stick. She knew I was made for worship and joy, and she wasn't going to let the enemy steal my identity. These were the moments I wasn't becoming something else; I was just able to find reprieve in who I was created to be. Even if these moments of escape weren't much, they were what I needed to keep my heart beating inside of my withering body.

I was no better off than before, still struggling greatly with my eating disorder. I was hopeless of this cycle of self-hatred ever ending in a relationship in which I was never affirmed. Even the close relationship my brother and I once had was now gone as he was moving out and pretty detached from us as a family. He was 18 and plotting out his own journey. To top it off, my parents were in a very tough season themselves, both relationally and spiritually. My parents split up for a season, my mom moved out, and I was devastated. I knew she wasn't leaving me, but the rejection I faced as our relationship crumbled was very personal.

I didn't know up from down, and my moral compass began to be influenced more by feeling and emotion than conviction. I had traded my desire to save myself for marriage for a fleeting moment at my boyfriend's house, eager to keep up with the ever-shifting pressure of dating someone older and desiring to be desired.

I was 17, a senior in high school, and all hope for marriage—for that happy ending—was slipping away. I hated myself, and I hated my life!

One night we played a show in a small all-ages club in Keizer, Oregon. I remember my long frizzy hair was pulled under a baseball cap, and my main goal of the show was to make eye contact with no one. We weren't playing happy music; the whole band took a dark turn as we were all in the middle of some confusing times. I was too nervous to interact with people after the show, but the guy who had booked us managed to figure out a way for us all to connect after the show. My dad was still in the band with me, so everywhere I went, even in new places, I felt an element of safety as my dad was always with me. He didn't really relate to me as a dad but as a bandmate. Out of the crowd emerged a boy that I had never met. He had never heard us play but was really into music and loved our band from the first song he heard. He wasn't the type that I was used to. He was cheerful, slender, and not afraid to tell me that there was just something very appealing about this hidden girl beyond the hat.

I was so confused; I was dating someone else. We had been planning a future together. I knew I wasn't happy, but I also knew that at a man's side was the only place I felt I could find value. Yet here was someone who told me the most astonishing things about myself, like he liked my feet, he liked how I sang, he was mesmerized by me. Honestly, it made no sense to me. I couldn't even catch the attention of my boyfriend with my face, much less my feet.

I was allowing this relationship to take on priority over my actual real relationship with my boyfriend. This boy was around my same age. We were both seniors in opposite schools. It felt so good to be around someone who was my own age. He got the school drama, and I wasn't trying to play older than I was. I knew what I was doing was wrong, but this black hole inside of me craving love and affection thrived off the attention. It wasn't long before I would find myself in bed with this boy, living a life I wasn't even clear was my own. I was staying late at his house, lying to my boyfriend and my father about what I was doing. I hated myself even more for the person I was becoming, but I couldn't stop the bleeding myself. This boy was no more than a distraction, but he was also the only one who made me feel seen and worthy of love. I was lost in never being pretty enough, and he would shower me with compliments on my beauty. I was living two different lives but also had no idea how to escape them both.

The guilt quickly caught up with me, as I hated to lie, and I began to run back to God with everything inside of me. I had taken a break from church up until that point. There was a nasty church split, and my parents, along with a rather large group, left the church. I wasn't sure why everyone was leaving, but since my parents were leaving and the youth group was pretty much nonexistent, it made it easy to leave along with my family. After everything I had done and the way I found myself living my life, I was very eager to get back to some sort of church. I knew Jesus truly was my only out, but I also knew there was no way I could be totally cleansed until I confessed.

So, I did. I told my boyfriend my secret! I sadly wrote a farewell letter to this boy that I had been fooling around with and made myself a promise to fix my broken relationship. Guilt works in strange ways. The very relationship I was totally fine putting on the line to feel loved somewhere else was now the one thing I was willing to give my whole life to protect! Shame covered my soul as my only goal in life was now to prove myself trustworthy to God and my boyfriend.

Before long, I found myself in the back of a van, parked beside some hiking trail off in the gravel. There was no beauty around me, just a picnic dinner I had prepared and a glimmer of hope—a proposal!

I was 17 when he asked me to marry him, and despite knowing better, I said "Yes!"

My parents weren't happy, but there wasn't anything they could do about it. They begged me to slow down and just give myself some time. I didn't need time; I already saw what I was capable on my own, and I wasn't going to live one more second of my life alone.

So, when most seniors were planning out their final year of high school and preparing for college. I was frantically finishing school so I could graduate early, working almost full time, and planning my wedding.

It was eight days after I turned 18. The day I was to be wed. My mom made my dress despite the hard turn our relationship took. In that season, I no longer felt safe opening up to her about anything happening in my life. My dad was the one I went to when the guilt of losing my virginity became unbearable. He was the one I talked to about my cheating, and he was the one that carried me through a tough season of trying to grow up way too fast. I never felt judged by him in any of my opening up. It was a new feeling to have such a bond with my dad. It was just he and I living in a two-bedroom apartment. I had much of his undivided attention, and as much as I should have slowed down the marriage plans because I was finally getting the love and attention I needed from my father, I still couldn't back down from my wedding date. Although as time drew close, I knew what I was doing was a terrible mistake.

The night before my wedding, my father found me in the bathroom getting ready for bed. He stared me in the eyes. I had never really seen my dad cry before. He told me he was sorry; he was sorry for not doing the best job at being my father, and he told me he loved me. I would have planned that wedding a hundred times over if I could hear those words every single time. They were the antidote to my aching heart. He held me there, as time stood still, and we both cried in one another's arms. This time it wasn't just me finding solace in his embrace, but he as well in mine.

The next day I was filled with the usual butterflies. Would everything go as planned? Would my estranged brother show up? Would I have the guts to go through with something that I knew was so wrong? It was only nights before when my fiancé had confessed that many things, stories, and mind games he had been playing for a year were all lies. The lies were so elaborate, I couldn't even sort out what was real or a lie with him anymore. He managed in a crying mess to convince me that he was sorry, but the truth was I didn't even know the person I was marrying. I was too afraid of letting everyone down to back out this close to the wedding, though.

The guests had been seated. The pastor and my fiancé were at the altar waiting for me. My father found me in the back of the church as the music began. The tears that had found us the night before found us again. He looked me in the eyes and said, "You don't have to do this! I will walk you right out the backdoor and cover for you!" The strength I had found to make it through that day all streamed out of my eyes as the walls around my heart crumbled. On one side stood the love of my father that I had always yearned for. A father who would fight for me, protect me, and honor my heart. On the other side, a man who I had begun to dream about a life with but felt no safety, love, or honor with. I was afraid and confused and did the only thing I knew to do. I told myself I was strong enough to go through with it. I mean, after all, how bad could it be?

My dad and I silently walked toward the door. With each step we took, the tears turned more into a river of healing for my broken heart. God showed up in that moment for me. He used this river to saturate the desert of my heart with love and acceptance. If only it stopped there.

We walked down the aisle, both crying, and I don't mean that silent tears were falling but the full-on ugly cry! It was a good thing my fiancé forbid me to wear make-up because it disgusted him; otherwise, I would have been a black-eyed mess! There wasn't a dry eye in that room. So many thought it was tears of joy and love that were streaming down our faces, not tears of fear, regret, and healing between my father and me. People later would say they could feel the love of the Father in the room like they had never experienced before in a wedding. I just knew I felt the love of my father like I had never experienced. This moment—this wedding—was about to cost me everything!

My lips said, "I do!" as my heart screamed out one final plea: "Don't do it!"

5

The Beginning and End of My Marriage

It was the second night of our honeymoon; everything should have been perfect. Well, that is, if anything was normal about this relationship. I should have spent the first days of my honeymoon lost in love and intimacy. Instead, I spent the evening begging my now husband to please talk to me and explain why he had no desire to be physically intimate. Shouldn't this have been the highlight of our honeymoon, not the low point?

As I sat and sobbed, all remaining traces of worth were rinsed away with my tears. All I could hear running through my own head was, "I knew it! My parents were right! What the hell was I thinking?"

How was I going to remedy this mess? I mean, I made vows that I intended to keep, but at what cost? Then I quickly went into chameleon mode. I knew I had what it took to be an amazing wife. I had planned for this role for almost half my life. It didn't matter that I didn't have the perfect husband. I could gain what I needed by being perfect.

I quickly learned to cook exactly how he liked. I cleaned every spare moment I could. I was lost in painting our new house and setting up a home. I was so busy trying to become perfect myself that I barely had time to fix how out of control our marriage had become. We weren't physically affectionate, we rarely hung out, and we were fighting a lot. I'm pretty sure we were both miserable. All I could do was maintain my level of control, and that's what I did.

My eating disorder was at an all-time peak. When I wasn't starving myself, I was binge eating and taking laxatives to chase the shame and guilt I felt for eating. My husband knew very little about my eating disorder. And this new habit I was forming, I made sure to hide from him. I was convinced the reason my husband didn't desire me physically was that I was too fat, and if I weren't fat, I would be pretty. And if I were pretty, I would be desired and worthy of love.

He took a new job, which became a new career path. He had always worked for his grandfather at his radiator shop. This was a new position at Oregon Youth Authority, something that, if he stuck with it, he could really have a career, which I think he desired. He was at the age of knowing his life was going somewhere really mattered. I was hopeful that a new job and new goals would put him in a better place. To my dismay, he instead was fried at the end of long days, turning to drinking more and more agitated than normal. While our weekends used to be spent together, I was now left alone for days on end, it felt. He worked a swing shift, so he left for work while I was at work and got home from work after I was already in bed. The worship band in which we both once served that connected us was something I did on my own, along with everything else that I did on my own.

For months the perfect wife in me just let it all go. I covered for him to all our friends and family. I don't think I really had anyone fooled. My parents could sense in my mood that things weren't good. Even Peggi knew things were off. I would barely reach out as I knew she would see right through me. I probably was a bit relieved to not have a partner at my families get-togethers as I know they would have seen right through my fake smile and past my baggy clothing hiding the frailness beneath.

Holidays, important celebrations, and anniversaries passed. Nothing could make him love me, to see me, to stay home and just spend time with me. He didn't marry me, he married his job, and if I played the "wife card," I was angrily dismissed and threatened with divorce. Every fight ended the same, him promising to divorce me because it just wasn't working. It's not like he had reasons for it not working; I think it just wasn't working, and he was tired of fighting about it. His way to control the situation was to threaten me with divorce because he knew how afraid of divorce I was. I would not have a failed marriage!

One dark night I sat in our kitchen; we had just gotten into another huge fight before he left for work. There was no resolve, no peace—he just slammed the door, and I was left alone, again. I was at my end; there was no hope left. I had tried to be perfect to gain love. I had managed to neglect everything about my own needs to be found worthy of attention. Nothing worked. I couldn't keep this going any longer.

I grabbed a kitchen knife and began cutting my wrists. The pain on the surface of my skin didn't even match the pain I was trying to kill inside of me. It wasn't fair. This couldn't be my life. How did I get here? One last slice, and the pain was too much. Blood slowly started dripping down my wrist, and I knew I was in deeper than I could handle. I wrapped my wrist in a kitchen towel, ran to the living room, and threw myself on the floor.

My wounds weren't deep enough to require medical attention but deep enough to scare me. I lay on the floor in a fetal position when I felt as real as the ground underneath me, a finger running down my spine. I lay there paralyzed when I realized a dark figure was in my room, and I knew I was messing with something that was far bigger than my 18-year-old mind could grasp. I believe it was a demon there for my life, but it also was a huge wake-up call pointing me to where I was heading if this whole thing played out how I thought it might.

Scared to death, I cried out to God. I knew I needed help. I couldn't do this on my own. Why was God so far away when I was at the end of my rope? In that moment, I didn't really care; I just wanted that demon gone. So, I begged and pleaded with

God. I told Him I would never try to take my life again. Even if I didn't feel my life was worth living, I wasn't going to try and control when I would be done living it.

The dark figure left my room, and I cried myself to sleep, alone.

In the following weeks, I found a new job at a local coffee shop. I had been working for years at the YMCA Before and After School program, but I needed to mix it up a bit. I had always loved the idea of working for a coffee shop. It was a lighthearted job, and I enjoyed the constant interaction with customers. It was a welcomed change from the drastic, lonely lifestyle I was living at home.

One afternoon, a local studio engineer came in, and we began chitchatting as I was serving him his chai tea. I was quite certain he was flirting with me, but I didn't care. He flirted with everyone. A few days later, he returned with his boss, Jack. They both let me know that they had come to meet the cute new coffee shop girl. I was flattered but also taken with the fact that Jack owned a recording studio. As it turned out, years prior, it was the studio that did all the CDs for the band I was in with my dad. They invited me to check out the studio, and within a couple of weeks, I was working there part-time. I didn't know how to do much, so I mainly did busy work. I ran errands and learned how to duplicate tapes. I just loved being able to work at a recording studio.

This seemed like the perfect escape from my life at home. I was doing something I loved but also around people who were constantly over the top with me in their verbal affirmations — everything from loose sexual comments to being complimented on a new outfit. I hadn't had this much positive attention in a long time, if ever. I knew it was all probably very inappropriate, but I didn't really care.

It wasn't long before Jack and I began flirting. Then the flirting led to real conversations about life. I felt I could talk to him about anything. Quality time was one of my love languages, and

I had been starved of it for so long. I could sit and talk for hours with him, and he would listen. I knew I shouldn't open up about my martial problems, but he felt so safe I could tell him anything. I found myself falling for him, and he for me. Much to our surprise, we started having an affair. I knew I had no place coveting what wasn't mine, and it wasn't as if I sought this out. He found me—literally, he came to find me in a coffee shop.

My assignments were home, job, and wife. What I saw in that season was much like King David as he gazed upon Bathsheba. She wasn't his to have, but the very idea of having her was enough for him to override his current assignment in his life. Love is a strong pull, but lust and finding value in someone are even stronger at times. I was starved for any value, for anyone who might show me an ounce of worth. Even though this relationship wasn't mine to have, I found more value in opening up and being seen than perhaps I had ever experienced.

He was everything that my husband wasn't. He was gentle and kind. He saw me. He encouraged me to run after my dreams and start singing again. He valued even the tiniest things about me. He found me beautiful and didn't struggle to tell me so, often. He made me laugh and begin to love life again. He loved the way I loved him and wasn't an endless supply of negativity and anger. He always made time for me, even if it was late into the night while my husband was at work and his wife was asleep.

It was one mistake traded for another. What was killing me at home didn't seem so unbearable when I was with him, but the shame and guilt I felt constantly was killing me in another type of way.

I began to pull away from church and even God as I knew there was no way I was walking in purity before the Lord. I knew what I was doing was wrong, but I also had no emotional intention of stopping it anytime soon. As far as I was concerned, this man was my lifeboat sent to carry me away. I felt worth from this married man who cared for my heart better than I ever had been cared for in the past, but I also knew I couldn't carry on like this forever.

It wasn't long before the guilt was eating me up inside, along with the anguish that I felt when the person whom I loved would always go home with someone else. It was a twisted type of pain. I may have stopped physically cutting myself, but this may have been worse.

The only way I saw of escaping this pain was to separate from my husband. I was living two lives, and they would never intersect. I had to make a choice one side or the other. Things between my husband and I continued to deteriorate. I think we both knew where our relationship was heading. I told him that I needed space to sort out my thoughts and feelings, and I wasn't wanting to live with him while I was doing that. He didn't know about the affair; he didn't really need to at the time. Our relationship was bad enough to call it quits all on its own.

I moved in with my best friend and lifetime sister. She didn't judge me for my separation as many were. She knew I should never have married when I did or to the person I did. I also wasn't being honest about my affair with anyone. I didn't need another opinion; I just needed some time to think. Time to weigh through what I would do. Would I miss my husband when I left? Would Jack leave his wife once he saw I left my husband? So many unknowns, and I needed time to tell.

I don't remember missing my husband once in that time. I know I felt guilty for being glad to be away. I knew I was feeling the shame of the possibility of a failed marriage at only 19, but I didn't miss the married life—the constant work of keeping someone afloat while you yourself were drowning. They say don't try to save a drowning person as they will unintentionally drown you in the process. This was my life. My husband was drowning. He had lost himself just as much as I had in the year and a half we had been married. Sure, he started a new career, but he lost touch with all his friends. He stopped playing drums, which he had loved. He pulled away from his family. He gained a bunch of weight due to depression and having no time for anything other than work. He had no idea how to save himself, so he decided I should be the one to save him, only to kill me in the process.

My heart was dying. I couldn't carry on. I knew that separation wasn't going to be the final destination, but divorce just seemed too painful. If I was 19 and divorced, it would just confirm everything that I feared about myself: I truly was trash, and everyone else would know it too.

In one last-ditch effort to say I did everything I should have done for my marriage, my husband and I began meeting with our pastors at the time. They didn't know us super well as neither one of us attended church regularly, but it felt like the most "holy" thing to do to council with pastors.

We sat there on their couch as he cried his way through most sessions. I was so emotionally disconnected that his tears were annoying to me. Plus, it wasn't as though I believed that any of them were real. I had seen this act from him right before we got married when he confessed all the lying he had been doing. This was the same mind game that I'd been living for years now. They, of course, fell for it and only saw my bitter shut-down heart. We didn't really share the extent of all our problems. There was no way to cover the year and a half of damage that was caused. There was no way to take them back to our wedding day, me knowing I should have never married this person. He cried because he knew he was losing me, but it's not like anything had been done over the last year and a half to "keep me." He was raised just like me. Divorce is bad, so a failed marriage wasn't something that he had set out for either. We both mourned the loss of our expectations of marriage more than we were grieving the loss of one another. This wasn't something either one of us could really articulate to our pastors, however. They prescribed what they felt was best and asked if I'd move home and give him another chance.

Reluctantly, I did just that. He still didn't know about the affair, but I knew that before God, if my life was ever going to recover, I had to see if these tears and remorse were real on his part. I made a promise to myself that if he was truly sorry and things were shifting, then I would end my affair and come clean, no matter what the cost.

Sadly, three days in, the same games, manipulation, mind games, and rejection were happening in my home. I couldn't call this home anymore, and I just stopped trying. I was done trying to perform for affection and to prove to myself and to others that I wasn't a failure. I was done trying to be perfect for him or cover up how miserable I really was. He knew something was different about me, and he bravely asked if there was someone else. In a catatonic way, I confessed everything.

The pain in his eyes killed me, but the relief I felt from the guilt, lies, and shame almost felt worth it. I was free from this burden, only to be blindsided by another. I hadn't thought through how this would play out in the other marriage that was involved in this whole sinful mess. I remember calling Jack and telling him that I had confessed everything and that my husband was going to be calling his wife in the morning. I felt so guilty for the terrible position I had put him in, almost as if all his own actions would have been my fault as well.

In the days that followed my confession, I moved out and back into my friend's house, for good this time. I had made up my mind. With or without Jack, I would never ever return to this broken life called marriage!

I sat at the kitchen table in my friend's apartment, journaling all that had just taken place, when the phone rang. I was hoping for it to be Jack as I still hadn't heard from him after dropping a bomb on his life, too. It wasn't him but another familiar voice of our pastor. He was calling me to let me know that he had heard of my affair and my decision to move forward with divorce from my soon-to-be ex-husband. I sat silently on the phone as he proceeded to tell me that God would always love me, but not in the same way because of my divorce. And God had plans for my life, but they wouldn't be the same now that I was a divorced woman.

I hung up the phone, and every fear I ever had about love was confirmed. It was all conditional, even with God. Despite this sick revelation, the truth that my mother had spoken to me years prior came resonating back through my soul. "People don't get to define my relationship with God, only God does," she told me. I may have known that the church is made of people, and people say and do dumb things. I couldn't hold that against God, but it didn't mean that I wanted to attend any longer. So, after a long hard battle to fight my way through religion, I decided church wasn't the place for me. I wasn't giving up on a relationship with God, but I was giving up on established religion. I had felt so judged by my pastor because of my divorce. I couldn't imagine having to tell any other pastor in any other church what I had walked through.

All within a week, I said goodbye to everything I knew my life to be at 19: my church, my job (Jack and his wife were going to try and sort things through, so I, of course, was fired), my marriage, and any friends that were both friends with my ex and I. This was no life at all.

It wasn't long before I had at least started a new job. It was at a music store. I had made some connections with people from when I worked at the studio, and they all put a good word in for me. It felt like a fresh start until Jack's wife made sure to come in, find me at work, and let my boss know what a whore I was. I was mortified. Here I was just trying to rebuild, and my past and actions kept showing up in every part of my life. There were a few other people from church and old friends that made sure to come find me at work and really lay into me about the type of person I was and how disappointed they were in me.

I still hadn't had the courage to tell my parents of the horrible things I was doing and had pretty much cut off my relationship with them as it was just too hard to be honest. They never rubbed it in my face being right about me getting married too young, but I still couldn't bear to face them. My life was in shambles, and this was not the person they raised. I was a disgrace to myself. How could I be seen as anything more than that to them? It wasn't long before the angry wife found my mom at her job and proceeded to drunkenly tell my mother what a whore and terrible person I was as well. So, whether or not I was ready to tell them, the universe had a funny way of doing it for me.

This wasn't the first, and it certainly wouldn't be the last time that I found myself at rock bottom. This time I couldn't just try to end it all, though. I made a promise to God not to try and end my life again, so here I sat, stuck.

A month after our separation, I rented a tiny little apartment. Three months passed as I still sat in my tiny apartment boxes, still packed. A manila envelope sat on my kitchen table. I barely had the guts to open it. I was too afraid to go meet with a lawyer, so my ex had drawn up all the paperwork.

As I read the word "divorce," my heart sunk. Every hope of getting married young, having children young, and creating a life that I had always dreamed of stared me in the face. And with one signature, all those dreams were voided. The enemy's voice was loud in my ear. All I could hear was what a loser I was, how no one would want me like that again, and how I let everyone down. I better never open up about all of this pain that I caused. This shame would steal my voice, my side of this story. If I hadn't had an affair, perhaps I would have felt less shame, but because I messed up so terribly, I couldn't allow myself to even tell people the pain that caused me to live the life I was living. I chose to leave that marriage with the clothes on my back, a few plates and cups, and my piano. Out of guilt, everything else remained in his home, and I forced myself to start completely over. After all, isn't that what I deserved?

Even then, underneath all the lies, all the hurt, all the shame, this still-small voice whispered inside of me, "This isn't the real me. It's time to prove to the world who I am. I'm not what you think I am. You'll see!"

6

Starting Over

Months passed, and I was well on my way to achieving this goal to prove to everyone, including myself, that I wasn't just a wasted life. I tried moving away from the town I was living in. Perhaps leaving my ex-husband and Jack and trying to start my life over again would be easier in a new place. I was determined to try my hand at college again. I had only made it through a term when I was newly married. Surely having a degree would prove to many that my life was heading in a worthwhile direction.

It wasn't long before my heart longed for the affirmation and connection that I found in my relationship with Jack, and it became clear that I was just running from that. I wasn't exactly sure where he and his wife stood as I knew they were going to try and work things out. I decided to take the risk and reach out. He let me know that they had decided to file for divorce. We both confessed to one another that we couldn't imagine not doing life together, so we decided to try dating for real this time. I moved back to my hometown, and we moved in together. He was not only a full-time studio owner but also a part-time musician, playing drums for many musicians around town. He also played for the late Larry Norman, one of the studio's clients. Larry Norman was touted as the father of Christian rock.

We were at Creation Fest, a large Christian music festival held in various cities across the United States. Jack was playing drums for Larry, and there was a familiarity that my heart craved. It didn't feel like church, yet everything about the environment was Jesus. The music was all for or about Jesus. Larry had known about our messy relationship but didn't judge us. He just loved us where we were at. This was something new and different from what I had previously experienced in the church.

The first evening of the festival, I found myself backstage while Michael W. Smith played for thousands of people. As the sun began to set over the gorge, it was like a gust of hope hit my spirit. What if this is where I was always supposed to be? I found myself lost in the music, lost in the beauty of creation, and asking God to please come like he used to when I was younger and show me a sign of his love, of his purposes, of his plans. I confessed my mess, laid it down, and pleaded with the God of the heavens to meet with me here. Before I even had time to object, there was a woman whisking me onto the stage with a candle in my hand, letting me know to pay attention for the right time to light my candle. All at once, the entire stadium lit up by candlelight, and Michael W. Smith began to play simply on his piano "Our God Is an Awesome God!"

What was even happening? I was confused about how I landed here on this stage amid this glorious moment, but I didn't care. This was God's sign. He moved heaven and earth, again, to show me his great love for me, his dying devotion to me. And in a crowd of thousands, I felt like that whole moment was orchestrated just for me.

I told God in that moment, "Whatever you have for me, you have my yes. Wherever you want me to go, I'll go! If you want me to leave this man I'm dating, I will! If you want me to follow you to the ends of the earth, I will. Jesus, you have my feeble, broken life! You have my *yes!*" Little did I know, but those three simple letters would become my life promise to the Lord.

The rest of the festival was a blur. We got to meet and interact with so many people from the festival that I would never have the experience to meet, much less talk to, on my own. It was strange to know you were a nobody, yet everyone treated you as if you were a somebody!

I came home from that trip so hopeful of a shift. I knew that living with my boyfriend still wasn't the right thing to be doing, but I also knew that I didn't have a job as I had just moved back from out of town and hadn't started looking for work again. I needed to figure something out before just making that big of a shift. I wasn't home more than a week before an old-time friend and woman I looked up to very much reached out to me and told me that they were moving to Kansas City as there was a movement of 24/7 prayer and worship that was being started. They felt called to go and be part of this radical group of people that would cry out day and night for the Spirit of God to come and move. There was this woman, Misty Edwards, that was leading worship at what was now being called IHOP, that I reminded my friend of. She felt I was just supposed to come, listen, and be part of it. This wasn't just a coincidence; this was God. Before I had time even to think it through, I was saying, "Yes!"

I packed my bags and let Jack know I had to go see what God might have for me there. He might not have been a Christian himself, but he was very supportive of my pursuit of God. I set out on the road with this family and their four children and kitten as we made our way across the United States to Kansas City. When we arrived, I found myself quite at ease in the prayer room. The endless praise and prayer, scripture, and new songs were like nothing I had ever experienced. Finally, a place that could feel like home.

It was easy to forget the person I had become in this new place. Everything about who I used to be came back—my love for worship and the Holy Spirit. It was exciting to think about reinventing myself, but no matter how much I tried to silence the nagging voice inside my head, I couldn't. I would wrestle for my worth inside my thoughts while worship played, and everyone seemed to be entering into new things with God that were off limits to me because of my sin, my shame, and my past. Perhaps, this is what that pastor meant when he said God's plans for me would be different after the divorce. Maybe what he meant was I would forever feel different than everyone else in God's presence. I would always feel like the beggar at the gates rather than the beloved inside.

Mixed with confusion and the reality of what was happening at home, I cut my time short in Kansas City. I resigned that even though it felt good to get away, I still had a life at home that I needed to return to. I know that God called me to Kansas City for a short time, and it felt as though the seeds that needed to be planted while I was there were, and so it was time to head home.

I dated Jack for another couple of years. Our relationship had some high highs and some low lows. I learned many things about my own desire to nurture someone in a relationship. What it was like to have someone gently handle your heart and your failures. I learned how to dream big and never doubt yourself just because you are different because it could be the one thing that might cause you to stand out at exactly the right time. Also, how dating your best friend was truly the best. I also learned that being left alone always triggered something deep inside of me.

Jack's band was very devoted to getting signed, which meant long hours, tour life, and sleeping on floors of people I had never met in L.A. I learned and saw things about the music industry that made me long for the safety of home. This also confirmed that I wasn't willing to do all that they were doing to try and make it in the music business. I went home from L.A. alone, and it wasn't too long before I was moving to the next available guy who "saw" me. And so, the pattern went.

It wasn't long before Jack and I broke up, and I was yet again jobless, homeless, and struggling to find which way was up.

I got a new job in Portland and had moved in with my aunt. She was always my landing pad. She would encourage me to come back to church and return to my first love in Jesus. It was as if I could understand the words she was saying, but I was listening through a fog. There was no more emotional draw to be part of church or even to spend too much time with God. Too much time with God usually meant that loud voice of condemnation would come screaming back, so it just felt better to my heart not to have any conversations with God at all. The conversation I had with God years prior at CreationFest seemed but a distant memory. I was in no shape even to try and sort through my messy life, much less have hope that God would even want me in His presence.

I was skin and bones and rarely smiled when I started my new job. I had been hired by a printing company that I had worked with for years while working at the recording studio. I was too timid even to introduce myself on my first day. This handsome, overly confident man came to my desk and introduced himself.

"My name is Max. Who are you? You new here?" His dark hair, green eyes, and preppy style caught my eye, but his personality was not my go-to. He invited me with some other people to lunch on my first day and every day for the next month or so. He would drive 45 minutes down to see me two to three times a week, always reassuring me that he would never date me because I didn't have enough going for me as far as my goals in life. To top it off, you never date someone you work with. He would always say, "You never dip your pen in the company ink." He felt just as conflicted by the whole interaction as I did. In one breath, he would talk to me as if trying to convince himself he would never date me, yet here he was calling and pursuing me. It felt like a whole other level of mind games, which I knew way too much about.

I wasn't his type anyhow. I was too skinny, my hair was too short, and the way I dressed wasn't his style in the slightest. I didn't have a good enough credit score. I was too lighthearted. Everything about him should have caused me to run in the other direction, but I was so broken—so lost in shame, guilt, and condemnation—that his lies actually sounded like the truth. I didn't have to defend myself against him thinking the worst about me because these were things I already felt. In a twisted way, I found solace in his rejection. After all, I knew that my years previously had proved I wasn't really worthy of love because of how badly I damaged those who loved me.

It wasn't long before he broke his own rules, and we began dating. When he finally kissed me for the first time, it was like I had somehow felt privileged that someone so much better than me would have stooped to my level.

What he lacked in real love, he made up for in the mental and emotional abuse. He spent the better part of our first six months proving to me that I was even more worthless than I knew. He would invade my space and my home while I was away at work, digging through my things to get involved in my finances and every piece of my life. He felt it was helping. I just felt invaded and terrified to be in an even more abusive relationship than my marriage. I longed for the comfort of my ex-boyfriend. I craved someone to see any worth in me as the last ounces of me were rung from my soul.

He had caused me to lose or reject all my friendships. He caused me to isolate and withdraw from my parents. I was on a deserted island of him and him alone. The worse he made me feel about myself, the more I realized I wasn't worthy of love or relationship with others at all, and I should be lucky that he even wanted me. All my old self-hate resurfaced but worse this time. He was a drinker, so I began to drink to cope with the pain. Somehow the numbing made me forget.

How did I get here? Living with an abusive man, a practical alcoholic myself, no friends, no family! I was miserable! I knew I probably deserved all of this, so I completely blocked out even the voice of God. I didn't pray anymore; I wasn't reading my Bible, and I certainly wasn't asking God about my life choices anymore.

There were a series of dark nights, and in the midst of all this turmoil, I knew that even I couldn't endure much longer. I reached out to my parents and finally really let them in on a bit of my life. Within moments they had offered me a place to stay to get settled and assured me things would be better if I just came home for a while. And so, I did. After a long night of drinking and not even coming home, I was blamed one final time for the poor way in which he treated me. I packed my bags and left. I moved back in with my parents.

I slept on an air mattress in their guest room. I'd go to work during the day and head straight out with a friend after work, where we would both drink too much, and I'd stumble home to try and hide from my parents my growing drinking problem. One night we went out drinking, and I awoke the next morning for work covered in my own vomit all over my mom's quilt, and I wondered if being home was going to be too much work. At least when I was living with Max, I didn't have to cover up how horrible my life was. The hiding was almost worse. It didn't matter how hard I ran; my mom always came chasing after me with her love and Jesus. We had a couple of rough years around the time she and my dad separated and my first couple of years of marriage, but we had repaired our relationship by now, and she was back to being my best friend. She would share with me beautiful things the Lord was speaking to her about me. She offered to pray with me, to just be a friend. I felt like a fraud. I couldn't tell her how far I'd run from Jesus; I couldn't tell her that his thoughts about me were wrong. I couldn't let her know how terribly I turned out.

So, I turned back to the abuse. I found myself celebrating a new job with Max and, a few weeks later, discovered I was pregnant. How had I sort of finally broken free from this abusive cycle just to go back, and this time to be trapped with a baby?

My whole world came shattering down. Being a mom was the only thing in my life that I ever really truly wanted. While others were planning on becoming doctors and teachers, I was dreaming of becoming a mom. Since kindergarten, that's all I really wanted in life. Even in and out of my darkest moments, I knew I wasn't a lot of things, but I knew that someday when I did become a mom, I was going to be a good one. I just couldn't believe that this was the moment in my life I was going to become one.

The second my eyes saw that line on the pregnancy test, everything changed for me. I sat on Max's balcony as we both tried to process this news together. We both knew that this was terrible timing, but both had been raised to make the "right" choice given the situation. Not only was abortion never an option for me, but raising the baby alone wasn't an option either. My life how I had known it couldn't be the same. I couldn't think about myself and my needs any longer. I had a baby coming, and that baby deserved a chance at a better life than what I was living. I somehow decided that I was going to move back in with Max, and my love for him would change him. I wasn't going to allow this baby to be raised without a father. I didn't care what I had to endure; this baby wouldn't suffer because of me.

I was filled with such excitement and anticipation to become a mom that the abuse barely phased me anymore. The nights Max would stay out drinking all night and come home to belittle me and curse our unborn child lost their sting as my dream of becoming a mother was on the distant horizon. He might have agreed that raising the baby together was the right choice, but it didn't mean that he was happy about it.

We got engaged, bought a house, and were settled a few months before I was due. My parents had stepped into full-time support for me during this time. I was opening up more to my mom every day. She would spend every evening with me walking. Rain or shine, we walked. It wasn't just for the health of the baby and me while I was pregnant, it was the lifeline I needed to keep myself alive. Sometimes when you are with someone who drinks, you drink just to block out how bad it is to be sober around that drunk person. Well, here I was, trapped with someone constantly drunk from the moment he returned home, and I had no way to escape it. So, just like earlier in my life, my mom became not only my escape but also my bridge to God. I started praying more, and I started trying to believe more.

June 15, we welcomed the most perfect baby boy I had ever laid eyes on into the world. It was a long 48 hours of labor, but every second of it was worth it. As I held my baby in my arms, I silently thanked God for his life. Everything about this perfect moment was tainted with the person I was sharing it with, but exhaustion and joy filled my heart. As I stared into my son's eyes, I knew he would be my new escape. I could withstand hell if he was with me. All the love that felt wasted on Max would now be poured effortlessly into Aidan, my son.

It took four days of postpartum exhaustion to set in before I was calling my mom, telling her there was no way I could raise a child with Max, like somehow it should have surprised me that he wasn't going to be a good partner or father. He would hold him at moments and say how proud he was of me for my great birthing skills, but when the baby would cry or I needed help cooking or being cared for, I dared not ask. He would nap rather than letting me nap while home for his paternity leave. It was clear that this baby would be his bragging right but my responsibility. My mom knew the depths of our disfunction but also knew that making any decisions in a state like this wouldn't be helpful. So, she did what every good mother should do: she prayed for me and asked God to do what only He could do for me, Aidan, and Max.

I was so deeply lost in love for my perfect little baby boy that the pain and heartbreak of my relationship barely phased me anymore. I had come to peace that this horrible relationship brought me this precious little baby and made my dreams of becoming a mother come true. So, in my mind, it was worth it.

I spent every waking moment with my son. It was like heaven beaming down on me as I beheld his perfection. He truly was a dream of a baby. He slept well, ate well, and was very peaceful.

As my maternity leave was coming to an end, I became deeply depressed and desperate. How could I leave my son? I wasn't prepared. I had been praying for a miracle, and God didn't come through. I just wanted to be a stay-at-home mom, to raise my son myself, to get to be a mom and not a stand-in for the sitter that he would be with him more than I would. Max wanted money and financial security. He didn't want to make the sacrifices for me to stay home or even go part-time. He wasn't even willing to have the conversation. His parents worked full-time; we would work full-time. That's all there was to it.

The weekend before I was to return to work, I headed over to his parents' house and had a beer with my son. I had pretty much given up drinking except for a beer or two over the week-end. Max went out golfing and drinking with a friend and ended up standing me up at his parents' house. By the time he returned home, I was in bed, and he was drunk. He came home like he often did in moments like this, entitled and angry if I crossed him or questioned him. This time I wasn't willing to back down, though. I was pissed, and I was tired of this lifestyle.

I charged into our bedroom, where he was trying to sleep off the booze, and started demanding answers to the pain and humiliation he continued to inflict on me with his drinking and disrespect. I was tired of my worth being found in how worthless he treated me. I wasn't fighting for the fact that he was out with his buddies anymore. I was fighting for my worth, and this time, I wouldn't back down until he saw the error of his ways. I smacked him on the chest, and he got up and began dragging me off the bed. I kicked him as he threw me to the ground. He called me names as he proceeded to call the police.

It was 9:05 pm, and the cops sat out front with me. My eyes were black from my running mascara, and I was trembling. They were inside talking to him and wouldn't let me back in even to check on our sleeping son. Apparently, I was the perpetrator because my last kick to his chest as he pulled me from our bed left a visible mark, and I didn't have marks from where he threw me down. They could tell he was very drunk, but still, when one person has a mark, they are the victim. They told me to sleep on the couch and just let him sleep it off as even they knew nothing good was going to come out of the evening.

I caught a glimpse of myself in the reflection of the front door as the red and blue lights of the cop car faded. I thought to myself, 'This isn't some trashy episode of *Cops*; this is my life.' This was the life my son was being raised in. This wasn't just a bad day to sleep off—this was hell, and I was choosing to stay living in it.

I crumbled on my son's floor. He was asleep peacefully. None of the drama had even affected his sleep. He lay there, the angel that he was, and I was the sinful, worthless mother that the cops were visiting on a Friday night. I began to silently sob. I begged God to please save us. I knew I wasn't worth a thing. Just like the prostitute at Jesus's feet, I had whored myself out to everyone and everything. I traded my worth. I traded my body for sex. If only I could feel beautiful and loved. I traded my dreams of being a beautiful mother in for this trash. I wasn't even worthy to beg for help at eye level. I understood why the women at Jesus's feet was down at his feet: because the torment of beholding something so beautiful would only cause you to recognize how utterly wretched you had become. I wasn't worthy of face-to-face, eye-to-eye contact. I wasn't worthy of being held, but maybe, just maybe, at his feet, these tears and this pain would find an end.

7

The Never-Ending Cycle

That was the night my heart died inside my chest. I shut off all feeling and, other than with my son and parents, I was numb. I was a robot completing tasks. My days held no meaning, and my nights were without purpose as I slowly began drinking again. I was a good mom. That was about all I had going for me, though.

I spent more time at work flirting and being flirted with than I did working. It was the one drug I could return to. I could always rely on some man somewhere seeing my gaping wound of a heart and having pity on me. And much like a dog that returns to its vomit, I would return to the one thing that would make me feel again: attention from men.

I had realized that Max would never change, and someone gave me some very profound, albeit worldly, advice: "It's better to have come from a broken home than to be raised in one." Those words pierced me. Here this whole time, I thought I was doing the "right" thing by staying with Max because somehow that would show our son the right thing. But really, I was perpetuating the cycle. It was going to be better to have his history be tainted than his future.

With that, coupled with a new work crush, I had all the confidence I needed to finally leave Max, and this time for good.

In a matter of a month, I had found a new place to live and let Max know that I was leaving. He may have believed he loved me and couldn't live without me, but he had seen me leave before. He knew I was serious this time and wouldn't be conned again. His biggest concern was paying child support, and I was happy to have him not pay for a thing if it meant he didn't fight me for 50/50 joint custody. So, we agreed on 75/25, and Aidan and I moved out.

New hope was bursting forth in my small two-bedroom apartment with Aidan and me. I could breathe again. I had a place to call my own, to make as safe as I wanted it to be. I got to call the shots on who got to enter and when I wanted them to leave. There was no verbal, mental, emotional, or physical abuse allowed in our little home. This is how it was always supposed to be.

Within the first month of moving in, I found myself wondering when my last period was. Maybe I was just late from all the stress I had been under in leaving Max. Maybe I had mixed up my dates, and I wasn't really that late at all. Maybe the new guy I was dating from work and I just hadn't been careful enough. Maybe… I found myself dreading even having this conversation inside of my own head, much less with any other human being.

This brings us back to where I started. I couldn't handle who I had become and the person I had to explain that I was to my parents that night when I told them that they were going to be grandparents again. So, I set out to try and fix every wrong thing that I had ever done to create this problem. So, surely moving back in with Max would be the best place to start.

After moving back in with Max, it was like I had almost created another version of reality that I was living in. I separated my heart from any emotions from my past with Max and was going to live in this new separate space.

I was a mom to a 16-month-old and trying to figure out how I was going to duplicate my efforts to do it all over again. Max may have been present in form, but I was essentially a single mom living in a home that wasn't even my own.

The Never-Ending Cycle

I was 20 weeks along when we went in to find out the sex of the baby. I don't know why I begged God for a girl, but I did. I feared this would be my last opportunity to have a baby so if I could just get my little girl, I would be over the moon. As I stared at the ultrasound picture, it was like God himself was directing the movement of the sonogram. There staring back at me was the perfect profile of my newest baby boy, and his nose was exactly like his father's and nothing like Max's. I knew I had been honest about the other man I had been with, but with this, panic hit my heart. This was no longer a possibility of something that I would have to work out; this was really going to happen. I was going to have to figure out how to have two baby daddies. I was going to have to live with the shame in my family for my entire life.

My fate was sealed, this baby wasn't a girl, and it wasn't Max's, but I hadn't the heart to say a word.

I was now working at an IT company doing inside sales. Work was my only escape from the mind game that was my home. My brother was working for the company, and I made a very sweet girlfriend that worked in the cubical right across from me—something I hadn't had in a very long time. The three of us would laugh for hours as we worked in our corner cubicle world together. I hated my job as there was no creative aspect to it. It was also super awkward working with the guy who I knew I was probably having his baby, but Max forbade me from speaking to him after I moved back in with him. I did love going to work every morning to get to be with them. It was the only part of my life in which I was myself. I would laugh uncontrollably and be nothing short of my ridiculous 26-year-old self. I wasn't trying to be anyone that I wasn't. I was just me, and it felt extraordinary.

So, when I caught the eye of a handsome, successful outside sales rep, Shane, at our company, I was in disbelief.

When I first met him, I was so convinced that he was the most arrogant guy I had ever met. He was just that type of guy. He drove a brand-new red BMW, he dressed super nice, and he clearly didn't need the attention of anyone because he knew he could probably have anyone he wanted. He was a mystery, though. He came across one way, but as his walls dropped, he became himself, which was totally different. He would send me flirtatious emails, and I would read them, looking over my shoulder, waiting for someone to jump out laughing at me, as if to say, "Joke's, on you!" This wasn't just some guy at the company, this was the top-producing rep at the company, and I was five months pregnant!

Our affair started there with no false pretenses. I wasn't trying to come up with a new version of myself. I was the office girl, pregnant and engaged, and he was the newly married sales rep pursuing me. It didn't seem to matter how terribly off the situation was. It's not like I was proud to be in the situation I was in, but my life was already so messed up that adding something else didn't seem that bad, especially if it meant some positive attention in my life.

It was the first time in my life since my first boyfriend that I was myself with a guy. I had literally nothing to lose. He had only ever experienced my goofy ridiculous nature, and yet somehow, he was drawn to that. He didn't need me to do or become something. I was already enough for him. He may have been attracted to me, and we may have slept together a few times before my stomach grew too large, but it wasn't about what he could gain from me physically. He just loved me—he loved my smile, he loved my eyes, and he thought I was funny and charming. He loved the things about me that I loved about me and that had been a very new thing.

Our affair carried me through my pregnancy. I would spend all day at work hoping to see him and connect. Then at night, I'd hope to be able to chat over email and sneak out of the room to text him. We were both living dual lives and deceiving everyone around us, but neither one of us cared enough to stop. I began to bring Aidan around him, and we spent hours playing at the park. He fell in love with me as a mother on top of everything else. If he had been single, I am sure we would have been married within the year. But he was spoken for, as was I. It was just the type of complication that I apparently craved. Max never seemed to suspect a thing. He probably welcomed my new mood and desire to always be out running errands, so I could sneak around or be at the park, as he could go out and be with his buddies or do his own thing.

As I was in the hospital giving birth to my baby boy, Ashton, I was still secretly texting Shane. I urged Max to go play poker with his buddies three days after Ashton was born so I could go meet up with Shane. All my heart wanted was to be with this man that loved me for me, yet his hand belonged to another. Yet my life was also evolving, and pretending to date someone was becoming harder and harder.

One day, Max called home and told me the results of the DNA test he had ordered—something I had already known in my heart to be true because of the sonogram. Shane helped me to get a couple of nights away at a local hotel to clear my mind and come up with a plan. Here I was in a hotel with a six-week-old and a two-year-old. The man I was engaged to was at our home, threatening to burn all my stuff if I didn't return with our son. The man I loved was at his home with his wife, building a deck, trying to carry on like business as usual all the while sneaking away to come check in on the boys and me as much as he could.

This was it; this was rock bottom, and I was done banging my head against this wall. This wouldn't be the life my boys would be raised in. This wasn't a vacation in a hotel, this was a nice shelter, and I was still running from the truth of my life. I was with a man I despised, I had two children that had different fathers, and I wasn't going to make either one of my boys suffer for it. I was in the middle of a messy affair, and I was way way too old to be acting so foolish.

This wasn't my breaking point; this was my reality check, and I was done staring back at myself in the mirror. I wasn't ever going to be able to look myself, much less my children, in the eyes if I didn't start growing up.

It was time for me to come clean with the man at work about Ashton being his and begin the process of figuring out how Ashton's life would look in the face of all of this. He welcomed his new son with open arms and was very excited! We had only dated a few weeks, and I hadn't been able to talk to him while being with Max, so it felt strange telling someone who felt almost like a stranger that we would be tied together for the rest of our lives through this sweet little boy. It was terrifying knowing very little about this person and how we would try to raise my sweet boy together. Another very hard reality check.

8

Get Home

Three weeks after our weekend trip to the hotel, the boys and I were moving into a cute little house in a sweet little neighborhood across town from Max. Shane's wife had found out about Shane and me because the hotel charges came across one of their joint accounts. He was spiraling and needing to figure out his life. He wasn't totally honest with her when she found out and just swore I was some person at work that he was having pity on because of my hopeless status and needing help.

She bought it for some time, but he was also being watched like a hawk. So he felt that until he had a better idea what he was going to do with his life, he should just take a break from seeing the boys and me to figure his life out. It was hard to be alone, but it was also everything I needed. I got to be the mom I wanted to be to my baby boys and to try and retrace the steps of my life to figure out where I had gotten so off track.

After a long hard eight months of Shane going back and forth with what he wanted for his life, he tried sorting things through with his wife. But in the end, they separated and eventually divorced. I was going back and forth with the idea of trying to figure out if I wanted to date Ashton's father. The idea seemed good, but we had very different perspectives on life, family, and God. Although I knew I wasn't walking with God, I also knew this was yet another step in the wrong direction. If I tried to start a family with Ashton's dad, I think we both knew we would be doing it for Ashton's sake, not for love and longevity. Shane and I both arrived at the place where we realized that the only way we were going to ever be able to live with ourselves was to see if we could live with one another. No one else in the way, just Shane and me. We were like magnets drawn to one another since the day we met and had caused ourselves and many others much pain in trying to resist the temptation to be together. It was time to take the leap of faith.

Shane bought a new house, and the boys and I moved in. We lived as if we had just gotten married and were establishing a life together. We picked out colors for the boys' rooms, and we bought new furniture together. We knew that finally we got to be together, and this life we were establishing was going to be bliss.

For quite some time, it was. Inside our perfect home, we were enjoying the nuances of coming together after all this time and the boys' split schedule with their fathers. There was still a lot of swirling drama around us with friends and family due to the fallout of Shane's marriage. All of Shane's friends were also very good friends with his ex, so socially, it was very awkward. There were things Shane was invited to, but I wasn't because his ex would be attending as well. We tried as hard as we could to keep the drama from touching our perfect bubble, but it was hard. We began to turn on one another in moments of pressure. I was realizing my prince charming had some issues, and he would realize I was no Cinderella.

I was in the middle of two custody battles for my boys. One was settled peacefully, and as hard as it was, I had to realize that I was only going to be able to have Ashton 50/50 with his dad. I knew this day would come, but it still broke me that because of my messy life, I would miss so much of Ashton's life. The battle with Max wasn't going so smoothly. He found no need for joint parenting, and as much as mediators and judges tried to convince him that two parents working together as a team for their children would be best, he insisted that absolute separation was the only way. This not only meant that he didn't want to discuss a thing about Aidan's life with me, but he made sure that Aidan knew he wasn't to bring me up while around his father. He would remove any trace of me from the moment he had Aidan at his house to the second he left. Aidan wasn't allowed to talk about me, call me, or mention any parts of his three-year-old life at my house.

The tension that was building deep within Aidan was causing deep anxiety and torment. He would wake up every Wednesday panicked, wondering if this was the day his dad would pick him up after work. He would spend the day in agony waiting for Max to pick him up, and as soon as the doorbell rang, he would start screaming and crying. We would have to document each encounter as "proof" to the courts that Aidan didn't want to go to his dad's. It would also highlight Max's refusal to co-parent.

It was torture to be part of. It felt like the cruelest thing you could do as a mother, but until the judge ruled in my favor, I had no option but to keep sending him for his weekly visit. Even the one night and every other weekend were more than I could bear.

Shane and I could pretend we were still dating on those nights, and that was nice. He wasn't the boys' dad, so the break for him was needed. He didn't just take on dating me but also raising two boys, and as well as he handled it, the break was still welcome.

One Saturday evening, as we were heading to dinner, my phone rang. It was Max. He informed me there was a huge fight between himself and his fiancée about ready to take place at his house, and he was dropping Aidan off. I told him I wasn't home at the moment, and he let me know that I had 20 minutes to get home, otherwise he was leaving him at the door. We raced home just in time for Max to be letting him out of the car and sending him inside. I had Shane get Aidan inside, as I was about ready to give Max a good talking to, when he informed me he was done being his father. He told me he'd sign all the paperwork and have it filed with the courts. He was done being "that kid's father," and he drove off. My heart broke for Aidan and the rejection he had encountered not only in that moment but how it would affect his whole life. Yet, my heart was so relieved that this court battle would be over. I would never again have to see my son pulled from my arms, screaming for me not to let him go.

Unfortunately, for Shane and me, our perfect little arrangement for a kid-free dating life was over. I lay in bed staring at the ceiling that night as sleep eluded me. The storm pressing in on Shane and me was already starting to erode our fairytale foundation. How was this going to affect us now? It wasn't that Shane had issues with the boys; it was just a lot for him as an only child, never having been around kids before, to go into full-time "dad" mode.

I got let go from my job as I wasn't making my performance goals. With all the drama surrounding Max and Aidan, my mind was always at home when I was at work, and then when I was at home, my mind was worried about work. I wasn't fully present in either place, and eventually, my boss let me go. Shane and I discussed me doing what I had always dreamed of doing: staying home with the boys, and so I did. Shane and I were fully playing house, and the lack of marital commitment was beginning to weigh me down. I was fully reliant on Shane, and so were my boys. We were starting down a path that, if it didn't work out, the boys' lives would be drastically messed with.

I decided I would become the perfect housewife and stay-at-home mom. It was a transition, that's for sure. After only wanting to be home with my boys for so long, I quickly began to realize how much of my worth came from holding down a career and being a mom. Shane was becoming overwhelmed by this very new, real way of living as a full-time "dad." The constant of children in our home, eating where the kids wanted, watching shows the kids wanted. Having to consider me and the boys before making plans and not just being able to go and do the things with his friends that he wanted. Mainly though, it was having to share my attention and affections that wore him down the most.

We began to bicker more than usual; we began to drink more than just on date nights, and then the bickering didn't just reveal the pressure we were both experiencing but the resentment that was mounting on both sides.

That Halloween, we went to a friend's house for a neighborhood party, and Shane drank way too much and ended up sleeping on some guy's couch. I had to find my way home because he was so out of control. My dreams were crashing in. This soulmate that I was sure was going to fix everything about my life was turning out to be no different than every other man I had dated. I found myself sinking and stuck again. I was becoming angrier with him for not meeting my expectations of him as a boyfriend or stand-in father for the boys. I would nag at him and start fights to try and get some sort of validation or movement in the right direction.

It was the holidays, and no one likes to break up or take time away during the holidays. Often, denial is the greatest over the holiday season. I spent the evenings drinking and drowning out the impending doom that my life and the boys' lives were about ready to transition all over again because I couldn't stay in this type of relationship.

Shane and I and the boys went away with Shane's friends to celebrate New Year's. I hated going away with Shane's friends, but this was their New Year's tradition for years. They would all rent a big house on the mountain and stay together over the holiday. None of them had kids, and they were all still very close to Shane's ex-wife. I felt like I was constantly having to prove to everyone why Shane left her for me, like I had to show them I was just as great or had to justify who I was in comparison to her. Then to top it off, the fact that we weren't really doing well just sounded exhausting.

We spent the first evening drinking and pretending away. I found myself sinking. I couldn't do this. I went upstairs to take a shower to try and clear my mind. As the hot water beat down my once again frail body from not eating, I knew I didn't have what it would take to keep going. Then as clear as I have ever heard God speak, I heard Him say, "Your time is done. Get home!"

One might think this would have startled me, but it was like that tingling that happens in your feet when they have been asleep. I began to cry, and my heart began to beat inside of my chest again. This was my savior coming for me. It wasn't a man; it wasn't going to cost me my worth or my body this time! I hadn't heard God's voice in so long, it didn't matter that it sounded serious and stern. It was my Father's voice, and I knew the grace had lifted for this lifestyle.

I don't know what motivated the prodigal son to come home, but I knew that hearing my Father tell me to "get home" was enough for me to start the journey toward home. I didn't know how I was going to do it, but I couldn't stop this blood that had begun to flow again. I knew this was a matter of life and death, and He was presenting a choice.

I sat there rambling with excitement and nervousness as I waited for Shane to come into the bedroom. I knew what I was about ready to tell him I was going to change everything for him—everything for us—but I knew I couldn't back down.

As he entered, I started the conversation with, "I know why we've been arguing so much!" Much like any male desperate for the solution, he was so excited to hear what I had figured out. That may have been the last look of excitement on his face for the rest of the conversation. I went on to tell him that I had made some realizations and these things would affect us, but in no way was this an ultimatum. I then proceeded to tell him that despite the way my life currently looked, I was a Christian. I loved God, and I hadn't been living like it for some time. I went on to tell him how I needed a "godly" man to help raise my boys, and I couldn't just playhouse anymore. I wanted to go back to church and try to salvage what was left of my faith. When God said, "get home," it became clear the things that I would have to give up, change and sever altogether in order to get fully back to Him.

Shane stared back at me as if I were speaking Chinese. He had no gauge for this type of verbiage. Godly man—what did that even mean? Church? Wasn't religion and church for weak people? He had no gauge for any of this.

He had few questions, which was very rare for him. We never really had conversations about God. We talked about faith, maybe a higher power was mentioned, but he had no idea about my deep history with the Lord. Not that I could have blamed him. Even I wouldn't have ever been able to believe that someone with my rap sheet believed in God.

We agreed we would continue talking about this, but I reiterated that this wasn't an ultimatum. You can't make people believe in God to be with you. I knew that from previous relationships.

As bedtime approached, I felt hope for the first time in years, and not a fading hope but something solid that could withstand the storm. We went to bed and quickly began to argue about the plans for the following day. Shane wanted to go skiing with his friends, and I knew that meant that I'd be left home with the boys. I knew I couldn't go with them, and I had just opened my soul up to him the night before, so I just wanted some reassurance or at least further conversation rather than just being left with the boys for the day in this house with all his friends. I was so tired of being the last thing on his mind in that way, and with his plans, I started a rip-roaring fight.

The next morning, I decided the boys and I would make the trek home alone. I knew I wanted Shane to fight for me to stay, but I also knew that he wouldn't. We would fight, but he would just disconnect the harder I pushed him, causing me to feel more rejection. I was done fighting him to stay with me. I knew God was calling me home, and I couldn't wait around any longer.

9

Returning to Church

It was New Year's Day. Not many restaurants were open, and most of them were filled with people nursing hangovers. Shane had caught a flight home as the boys and I had left the day before, and we found ourselves together trying to sort through the puzzle pieces of our relationship. Shane was confused, and I had no real answers. I had never been this far away from God before, and I had no idea how I was going to "get home." I wasn't even sure how one recovers after messing their lives up quite so much. We knew that what we shared was worth something, however, and although it was more confusing than clear, we were going to try and walk down this path together.

Shane agreed that he would go to church with me. He wasn't making any guarantees, but he was at least willing to try and preserve our relationship if this is what I required moving forward.

We found a local Vineyard church right down the street from where we lived. I had been raised at the Vineyard, which at the time was a nondomination movement that included belief in the Holy Spirit as well as Jesus and God the Father. So, I at least knew that I believed in the things they were teaching.

The first few weeks were fine. Shane was totally taken by the charismatic nature of the church and was often distracted and concerned with how strange all these people were. Worship was the hardest for him, but it was like breath inside my lungs. It was like the Earth stopped spinning just for me, and I found myself hiding my tears as they streamed down my face.

"At the cross, you beckon me. You draw me gently to my knees. And I am lost for words, so lost in love. I'm sweetly broken, wholly surrendered."

This song washed over me day and night. I didn't know what it must be like to be sweetly broken because I wasn't sweetly broken. I was crushed against the harsh rocks along the seashore. I was like a ship that became shipwrecked. I wasn't gently drawn to my knees, I was forced to my knees out of shame and guilt. The words and melody haunted me as I knew I was being invited to live on the other side of this. What would it be like to feel beckoned? To fall to my knees out of deep love and surrender, what would sweetness feel like to my war-torn soul?

I was all in to figure out the answer to these questions. I was all in to read my Bible full-time again, get the kids into Sunday school, and dedicate my life fully to Jesus again. My full commitment, however, was met with Shane's doubt and skepticism. How could I believe that the Bible was real? Did I actually believe there was a giant boat and a tower to heaven? What type of idiot believes this stuff? These were the questions that Shane would ask while trying to sort out his own feelings about this new church and God thing. I would ask him to please find someone from the church to talk to. Get together with some of the guys that had made efforts to help us feel welcome at the church we were at. Ask them the hard questions because it was too hard for me to be establishing my faith with someone constantly trying to poke holes in it.

Shane was raised with no belief in God. Both of his parents were raised in different strict religious homes and disliked the church greatly as a result. So, they vowed to raise Shane with no views on God at all, so he literally had no concept of faith, the Bible, or Jesus. Every part of this was like learning a new weird language. Shane believed that only weak, poor, and desperate people needed God. He had always been wealthy and successful, so he saw no need for God.

The chasm grew between Shane and me. I no longer had the grace to be with someone not running after Jesus, and there was no way Shane was all in for something that made no logical sense in his own mind. We came so close to something so beautiful, but I knew I could no longer choose men over God. God drew a line in the sand of my life that New Year's Eve, and I wasn't going back. Shame might be the ruler of my heart still, but at least my heart was beating again.

The boys and I moved out, and Shane and I broke up. I was on track for learning how to learn how to do things right. I was far from perfect, and many of my old ways and ways of handling things were still intact. But I chose obedience, and that felt like a big step in the right direction.

Just like magnets that repel and attract, that's how Shane and I always had been, and this was no different. As hard as we tried to just stay away from each other, it was hard. We would text each other in one moment to say we hated one another for ruining our lives, and then in the next, we'd express how much we missed each other. He would still text me about random faith questions in the midst of trying to carry on his "normal" life, and I would challenge him on who he really was as a person and how he could experience a little bit of truth just to reject it. We would agree to not talk for a while, just for one of us to break down and reach out to the other. It seemed that no more than a week would pass over this time period that one of us didn't end up breaking our own rules to communicate with the other.

It was six weeks into our breakup, and Shane called after having a strong conviction that so many of the things I had said about his life were true. I had pointed out his selfishness, his self-centeredness. We had many conversations about his love of wealth, success, and things and how none of that would add up to anything when he died. He had just as many issues using women for validation and as his savior, all while missing the fact that he needed a Savior. He had come to realize over our separation that there was more. He knew that he didn't know what that more was, but he knew he needed God and wanted to join the boys and me at church.

We started attending church, and things began to click in a different way for Shane. He began to own his own faith a bit and could feel the pull of the Holy Spirit on his own. His questions didn't just end at church, but he wasn't looking at things through such a distorted lens either. We began dating again shortly thereafter and became pregnant within weeks. On November 7, 2009, we were married. Our pastor performed the ceremony, and my dad walked the boys and me down the aisle as Shane vowed that he wasn't just marrying me but also becoming a father as well. There were tears this time, but not the ones filled with fear and pain. Rather excitement and joy. We had made it past the finish line and would be expecting our first baby girl together that April.

I'd be lying if I said the first year of marriage was good. It wasn't! It was brutal, and to be honest, I'm not sure how we made it. I was trying to wrap my head around all the pain I had lived through for so long, my own coping mechanisms, and the way I had felt hurt by Shane before. Neither one of us had an easy time letting our pasts go and would fight much like we had before. Just because we both now had Jesus didn't mean that we had anyone to teach us new tools of communication and how to truly love one another. You can give your life to Jesus, but fruit isn't grown overnight, just like good character isn't grown overnight. We probably wouldn't have made it past the first year without having a baby together and God. I reacted to conflict much as I always had. I was just going to need to earn love.

It was the lie that had followed me my whole life: what I wasn't offered in love, I could earn by doing. And what I could do was to become the perfect wife and mother. This was what I had always wanted, so it shouldn't have been too hard to walk in perfection to maintain peace in our home. I didn't pull out all my old tricks, but I pulled out many of them. I still hadn't confronted the lie that my weight and looks earned me love, so I began secretly starving myself again and hoped to gain a breakthrough on my own ground. I had always been unhealthy and underweight when we were together, minus when I was pregnant, so Shane didn't really understand the extent of my eating disorder nor my self-hatred.

No matter how hard I tried, no matter what I gave, I couldn't run from the truth. I just wasn't able to measure up. I couldn't run from the lie of religion that loves to keep us in bondage, telling us love was earned and based upon our doing. No matter how hard God tried to set me free from these lies, they were too entangled in my identity. Religion is like a vulture sucking dry the very essence of life, but lies and shame were keeping me from a deep relationship with Jesus. I wasn't sure how I was going to escape this cycle of lies, but I knew I had to.

10

Worthy of a First Dance

Right in the middle of my mess, God met me. We had started a home group, and no matter who came, we faithfully met every Wednesday night. Sometimes it was just Shane and I and my parents; other times, there were 15 people or so. Even though our home wasn't perfect, we were walking out our faith and trying to run after God the best we knew how.

This particular Wednesday night was different. Our friend Paul arrived late with a younger student from a school somewhere in Redding, California. We had been hearing lots about this church and school but hadn't met anyone from there. This small-framed girl from England beamed with joy as she walked into our home and expressed how much of the Lord's presence she could feel in our home. I was so touched as that was my only goal and aim. All other things were dim in comparison. If a stranger entered our home and felt God's presence, that meant the world to me. She instantly had my ear, and for some reason, I felt very at peace with her. It must have been at the Lord's lead, but I opened up about the guilt I was carrying and experiencing nightly about my children.

Sometimes it's called "Mom guilt," but this felt like more than that, I explained to her. I was carrying so much guilt and shame from the first four years of the kids' lives that all it took was pressing on the wound in my heart a little, and I would cave under the pressure. So, every night, that is just what the enemy would do. He'd apply pressure. He would replay my whole day, not through a lens of joy and pleasure but rather through the lens of everything I did to fail my children—every wrong tone, word, action, or motive. I would cry myself to sleep every single night, and some nights, the torment was so bad I'd pull Shane in on it too. Letting him know how miserably he had failed as a parent that day too. We would both fall asleep under this could of guilt and shame, both frustrated and angry with one another.

It was hopeless and hurt to my core, but I didn't have the strength to say "no" because, after all, wasn't all of it true? Wasn't I a terrible mother to have put my boys through everything I did? Wasn't I currently raising three babies from three different dads? I wasn't exactly worth defending. You see, the enemy doesn't need to reinvent the truth. He just needs a little to distort and throw back at us as failure. If we let him in, he will continue using that door until we close it.

As I exposed my deepest pain, this small girl asked if she could put her hand on my shoulder and pray for me. With more authority than any small person should have had, she commanded that thing to lift in Jesus's name. Something so deep lifted off my heart. The knife that was being twisted was removed, and a deep healing balm was being poured where the wound was. I could literally feel a weight lifted from my shoulders as she finished praying. I sat in my kitchen as she joyfully said goodbye and thanked us for allowing her a chance to come over and meet us. It didn't make any sense; she was thanking me! She had just partnered with God to remove one of the most painful knives that still remained in me from my past, and she was thanking me!

I went to bed that night, and for the first time in months, I fell asleep perfectly at peace. That lingering lie about me not measuring up as a mother never showed its ugly face ever again.

While my third baby, Amalia, was still young, I went with a group of youth down to Redding for a Jesus Culture conference. I was without children or a husband for the weekend. This was the first time in years that I had done anything apart from my family. I remember lifting my hands in praise, adoration, and thanksgiving. I remember every time they would ask us to "lift up our own songs to the Lord," tears would stream down my face, and all I could get out was "thank you!" I had no other words. It wasn't because God wasn't worthy of far more words; I just couldn't ever get past my thankfulness that He still loved me.

It was in that moment that the Father drew close and whispered the most profound words to me: "Stop thanking me for loving you!" I remember thinking that it wasn't God, at first. There was no way this was what God was saying. It must have been the enemy. I mean, I was doing what I knew was worship. This is how I was trained to worship at a young age and what set me free from bondage. This is how I most intimately connected with Jesus.

I was confused and concerned. I asked if the thought was God and heard Him say, almost amused, that He didn't need my constant thanks, just my love. I remember that feeling so foreign. As my mouth formed the words, "I love you, Jesus," over and over again, I realized how bizarre it felt to say those words out loud. It wasn't that I didn't love Jesus. It just wasn't how I was used to coming to Him.

I was but a used shell of a person for so many years of my life. Love wasn't the commodity that I was used for trading. Thankfulness was far easier for me to give and receive than love, and in this moment, I realized it had become my language with heaven. I knew I had very little experience with this new way of relating to God, but I knew from that moment that I was all in. Although thankfulness would perhaps get me through the door, it was love that was going to keep me inside.

Time passed, and as Amalia was approaching two, I was fairly convinced after I had her that I was good not having any more children. Shane had never really thought much about having kids, and now he was the father of three: two full-time children of his own, as he had adopted Aidan after we wed, and one that he was stepfather to. It wasn't too long after Amalia turned two that I got that itch again. This wasn't just the standard itch, though. There was something different behind this itch. God started sharing things with me about this new baby and the plans and purposes that He had for this baby. It made no sense to me, especially since Shane was still convinced that he didn't want any more children.

We went back and forth, forth and back. We prayed, debated, argued, and made lists, yet nothing shifted. One glorious morning, after being ten days late for my period, I saw that wonderful line. I was pregnant. I texted Shane while he was at work, and he came home with some flowers and a card that read, "Congratulations to you!"

It didn't take much to read that he was pissed. Clearly, he felt that I won and he lost. He wasn't sure that he would ever have children, much less three of them. He was content to leave it at three, and my desire for four just made him feel that I wasn't happy and satisfied with his compromise already. We stayed up the better part of the night arguing over the whole situation and him being angry with God for going against his desires and me trying to convince him that just isn't how God works.

The next morning, I awoke with him already up. My eyes were swollen from crying; they were the only thing to greet me with a lonely hello. I felt weird, but I also knew this was my fourth pregnancy, and none of them had ever been the same. I stood up, and blood began to gush down my legs as I ran to the bathroom. I sat on the toilet as I lost my baby. I didn't just lose my baby, though. I lost. I was angry at Shane. I blamed him for not wanting the baby, for the strain it may have caused arguing with him the night before. More than anything, I was angry with God; how could He do such an evil thing.

I didn't get dressed for days. I would wake up to be with my children, and that was it. I couldn't see past my pain. I couldn't look Shane in the eyes, and I wasn't willing to part with the idea that this wasn't his fault. One evening, as I wept before the Lord, I asked the question that usually has no answer: "Why?" "Why did You allow this to happen, God?" It was in that moment that God answered my question in a way that only He can. It wasn't the why, but it was enough to give me insight and direction, enough to give me peace.

God spoke to me of the importance of unity between Shane and me and that this battle of "winning and losing" was something that needed to be settled in both of our hearts. We needed to die to the idea that we were two individuals fighting for our way. Rather, we were two who had chosen to become one, and out of that place of unity and peace, all things should flow. I remember thinking back on our debates, our arguments, and the power struggle that was happening in our marriage, all to determine who might "win" the debate of children. I remember thinking, 'How could we bring a baby into this world under those premises?' I laid down my desires to control the outcome and trusted that if God had another baby for our family, it would be a gift from Him, and I would have to surrender the need to convince my husband whether it was God's will or not.

I wish I could say the surrendering was easy, but it wasn't. I was used to pushing and building cases for the things I wanted, especially if I felt the Lord was on it. Alas, we both agreed that we had a company trip that Shane had worked hard to earn. We would go on and pick up the discussion again after we returned home. It was on that trip that we were able to relax, take a step back and just enjoy one another without the pressure of making huge life-altering choices. Without the pressures of raising our young three children, without the pressure of two individuals, rather the two becoming one. I remember sitting in the water off the coast of Turks and Caicos, with Shane's company, enjoying the afternoon when Shane's boss asked us what was new and what we were doing with our lives next. It was then that I first learned God had done a work in Shane's heart, and he was willing to try for another baby. No one at the company knew of my miscarriage. I remember giving him a hard time for deciding to tell me in front of his boss that we wanted to try for another baby. It was his way of testing the waters, though—his was of coming to peace with the changes in his life—and I had to honor his process. Regardless, I was over the moon, and we agreed to start "trying" when we got home from our trip.

Here I was, three babies in, and I had no idea how to "try" to have a baby. I was so afraid that after setting our hearts in unity and on trying, I wouldn't be able to get pregnant. I read up on how to conceive and felt so silly that three children in, I was just now reading about the best time to conceive. Nevertheless, 12 days later, we saw that beautiful life-changing plus sign! We would be having our miracle rainbow baby, conceived in promise, intentionality, and unity. We named him Alijah: "Jehovah is my God."

I was living in the midst of my promise, with my four children, an amazing husband, and even having the opportunity to build our dream home. Yet my heart was still missing so much. I couldn't shake the feeling that my perfection earned me love and there was no room for error. I may have been released of 'mom guilt,' but that didn't help the constant striving that I felt like I had to do in order to "prove" to God that I was worth the second chance He so graciously extended to me.

I didn't feel I had to earn and prove myself only to God; it was with Shane, too. I often walked around defensive to any criticism. I was ready to break any time he complained about something around the house that wasn't being kept the way he would have hoped. I had become even more of a perfectionist and didn't realize how it was affecting me. I wasn't joyful and lighthearted, enjoying my life and my children. I was uptight and performance-driven.

When Alijah was two, I was in desperate need of a refresh. I needed to remember who Sarah was. Not the Sarah that was mom, not the Sarah that was wife or daughter, friend, worship pastor or leader. I needed to be reminded of who I was. A group of ladies decided to head down to a women's conference at Bethel Church called Wonder. I invited my best friend and my mom to join us. I was so not into women's events, but I loved Bethel and hoped that having my best friend and mom along would make it an extra special trip. We all packed my car full and rented a big house so we could all stay together. As it turns out, I wasn't the only one in need of some time away and to be reminded of who they were.

The first night was good. The worship and teaching were good, but nothing really stuck out to me. As the lights dimmed on the second night of the conference, I closed my eyes and became very aware of how much I wasn't feeling anymore. My heart was numb, and I was on autopilot. The stage lights bounced to and fro in the lids of my closed eyes, and tears began to stream down my face. How could I be sitting in a crowd of hundreds of women and feel so out of place? How had I become so isolated and unaware of my own pain? I had mastered the art of tending to everyone else's needs and hearts, but my own heart was dying from lack of nutrition itself.

In that moment, an image of Jesus appeared in my mind's eye. I had had visions before—this was nothing new—but not of Jesus. He walked right up to me, stared me in the eyes, and said, "You never got your first dance. You are worth a first dance!" I buckled under the weight of my own pain and tears and fell to the ground. Every image of my painful first wedding and marriage replayed through my mind. Every painful image of all the previous relationships that led to me finding Shane played, and even my wedding to Shane came to the forefront of my mind. Shane was too busy running around at our wedding, getting the music taken care of and making sure our guests were tended to, that he and I never had a first dance.

I had never felt worthy of someone slowing down enough just to dance with me, to just be with me and get lost in their love for me. I was always a bridge, a tourist attraction on a trip to someplace else. I was the much-needed rest stop that you stop at because you need something, but you never actually stay there just to be there.

I had learned to cover up my disappointment with excuses, and in that moment, all my excuses failed. Jesus had come not only to tell me I was worth stopping for and just being with, but what that meant to my heart was that He was saying I was worth healing! I walked away from the second night of that conference changed. Something shifted about how I could see myself because of this experience with Jesus.

Jesus's heart and plan weren't to keep me broken and fragmented, but He was very invested in seeing me become whole. He made me the commitment that He had come to heal my whole heart and that I was, in fact, worth it.

11

Returning Home

Shane has a very natural way, a gift even of connecting with people. Whether it was in ministry or his job, he was born with this fearlessness. Whereas I am shy and timid at first, he almost sees that first meeting as possibly your one and only opportunity, and he doesn't waste it. Since I have known Shane, we have had an opportunity to connect with so many amazing people who were just a few steps ahead so that we could almost ride in their wake before embarking on our own journey. Each connection has deeply impacted our lives, some for longer periods than others.

It was November of 2015 when we first met Ravi Kandel. We had seen him in the film *Father of Lights* by Darren Wilson. Then a friend met him and connected us. He was going to come stay with us as he taught a conference at the church we were attending at the time. It was in our kitchen that he told us we would have one more child, and Shane quickly rebuked him for saying such a thing. (Little did he know I was already debating in my heart with the Lord over having another baby.)

Ravi stayed with us for two short days, and my life was flipped upside down. He was deeply invested in seeing people healed from their pain and set free from their harmful thought patterns. I knew I needed to go through his six-week emotional healing course. It would be six weeks of a once-a-week call. It was long distant counseling, and it seemed like something I could make work, even with my busy life. God had told me I was worth healing, and an opportunity like this had never come along before.

I was terrified during my first call with Ravi. I sat in the Starbucks parking lot, too afraid to go in and be on the phone because I was already in tears before the phone had even rung. I was so thankful it was just a call and not on FaceTime because I wasn't holding it together even in the slightest.

"Why was I even doing this? Who does inner healing with a prophetic person? What was the point of me even sharing anything as he already probably heard all my dirt from God anyway?" So many questions streamed through my mind. Ten minutes passed, and no call. I was almost relieved to not have to go through it, and just as I was getting ready to head home, my phone rang. It was Ravi.

We got the small talk out of the way, and Ravi then asked me why I was doing these calls. I told him I really didn't know, but I knew I was broken and didn't know how to fix myself. I told him I was done trying to hold it all together and something about knowing I was worth healing and not knowing how to heal was almost worse.

As I mentioned, Ravi was prophetic, and he had actually told me many accurate things about my life, my children's lives, and many of our friends during the two days that he had stayed with us. I sat there just waiting for him to reveal to me what "Daddy" had said about me. He always referred to God as 'Daddy," and it felt so less than holy to me. It is almost insulting to the very glory that the name God could or should ever carry. Yet it was endearing, and it was that piece to a relationship with God that I was missing.

He started the sentence, "Sarah, do you know what Daddy told me about you before our call and about your past?" I shook as I awaited the embarrassment about ready to come my way. "Daddy said He isn't going to tell me anything about your past because He isn't here to expose you or shame you!" I sobbed in disbelief. Not only did God tell me I was worth healing, but He also loved me so deeply that He knew it was going to have to be different than anything else I had ever experienced in my life. He wasn't willing to break my trust in order to heal it. He wasn't willing to expose my sin in order to restore dignity. He was willing to let me be the author of this journey and restore dignity to myself as a person.

So many lies were washed away by this one simple act—this notion I carried that God was always focusing on my sin—and my past came crashing down around me. If God wasn't after exposing my sin, then maybe, just maybe, He was truly interested in my heart. He didn't just want this perfect slave and servant. He wanted me, and He was willing to show me in a very beautiful way by being so gentle and so kind. It meant the world to me to know how much He wanted me. He could have, in one fell swoop, exposed everything, made me whole, and sent me on my way. Instead, He was willing to let me take the lead on this journey and show me His love and gentleness, things I hadn't experienced a ton of.

"Dignity," according to the Merriam-Webster dictionary, is a seven-letter word meaning "the state or quality of being worthy of honor or respect." To me, I was never worthy of such a definition, much less the notion that I was worthy of my dignity being restored. In every relationship I had been in, my dignity was the first thing I had to compromise on to start that relationship. The fact that God was willing to restore my dignity by not leaving my backside exposed healed more inside of me than if I had magically been released from the ache and memories of my pain.

Where I was once apprehensive, I now found myself charging full speed ahead into my calls with Ravi. I didn't hold anything back and was finding this new part of me coming to life — a part of me that was once a slave to an evil inner voice and critic. It was the place where fear controlled me, swinging my moods from one second to the next based upon whatever lie the enemy whispered into my ear. I found a steady rhythm. For the first time in my life, my emotions were steady. Steadiness replaced my drastic highs and lows, and I was able to choose another feeling than the one that I felt. I was no longer a victim of my thoughts and feelings. Rather, I was becoming powerful.

My final call was late at night, and I locked myself into my husband's office, trying to hide from the kids to be alone with my thoughts. I had gone quite a few weeks not crying on my calls, and so I thought I was reaching the end of my pain. The well of tears perhaps had dried up, and I just anticipated hearing, "Well done for completing your course!" Man, was I wrong!

Ravi asked me to close my eyes and visualize my secret place with Jesus. He asked me to describe where I was in my mind's eye, and I told him I was at the beach. He knew the significance the beach held in my life because of my experience of finding God at the beach when I was a child. So, he wasn't surprised.

He asked me to visualize Jesus standing at the water's edge and what it was like to see Him and run to Him.

Everything inside of me stopped. I could hear the waves; I could smell the salty air and feel it deep inside my lungs. My breath went from shallow to deep as I tried to gain my composure. I had grossly miscalculated this last call, and before I knew what was overtaking me, it was like my emotions struck water inside a well that I never knew was there.

Even in my own thoughts, I couldn't approach Jesus. I would watch Him along the water, and here I stood hidden in the sand dune. There was nothing inside of me that could find the courage to approach Him. I couldn't speak, and it was no longer necessary. The last brick in my faulty foundation was crumbling, and there was nothing I could do about it. Every lie I had ever believed about myself came crashing down around me. Every lie that I had ever believed about God came down as well. My footing was no longer secure but shaky, and the only thing I knew that I knew was that shame had become my only companion. Shame was the thing holding me back from loving myself. Shame was the thing holding me along the shore when, deep down, all I wanted was to be able to run to Jesus and to know that He would embrace me.

I heard the Father ask me, "Are you ready to leave all of this behind?" The shame that had become my companion, the trauma and lies of my past, the idea of earning love. My heart began to race, and even though this cage became my home because it was familiar, I knew my heart was dying inside of it.

I didn't run to Jesus as Ravi had asked me to. Instead, I slowly walked. My shoulders rounded, and my face was hidden in my long, sea-blown hair. When I got close enough to Jesus's face, His eyes were as gentle as a still lake, but the intensity in which He embraced me was more powerful than a million seas. I was transported to being a kid, and my heart found its beat again, where pain, lies, shame, and guilt had been my lens. Love, dignity, and acceptance were now filling in all the blanks. Every moment I felt unseen, He showed me how He saw me in those moments. Every time I felt so far away from Him, He showed me how close He had drawn near. He was never angry and disappointed. He was still whispering His deep, perfect, unending love into my ear.

I had often heard the story of the prodigal son's return through the lens of the returning son.

> A man had two sons. The younger son told his father, "I want my share of your estate now before you die." So his father agreed to divide his wealth between his sons.
>
> A few days later this younger son packed all his belongings and moved to a distant land, and there he wasted all his money in wild living. About the time his money ran out, a great famine swept over the land, and he began to starve. He persuaded a local farmer to hire him, and the man sent him into his

fields to feed the pigs. The young man became so hungry that even the pods he was feeding the pigs looked good to him. But no one gave him anything.

When he finally came to his senses, he said to himself, "At home even the hired servants have food enough to spare, and here I am dying of hunger! I will go home to my father and say, 'Father, I have sinned against both heaven and you, and I am no longer worthy of being called your son. Please take me on as a hired servant.'"

So he returned home to his father. And while he was still a long way off, his father saw him coming. Filled with love and compassion, he ran to his son, embraced him, and kissed him. His son said to him, "Father, I have sinned against heaven and you, and I am no longer worthy of being called your son."

But his father said to the servants, "Quick! Bring the finest robe in the house and put it on him. Get a ring for his finger and sandals for his feet. And kill the calf we have been fattening. We must celebrate with a feast, for this son of mine was dead and has now returned to life. He was lost, but now he is found." (Luke 15:11–24 NLT)

It wasn't hard for me to put myself in the son's shoes. I had sinned against heaven and my heavenly Father. I often wondered how the prodigal son felt as he saw his father running toward him. He had no idea that he was about ready to be treated like the son he had always been, not the mess he had become. I could only have imagined that he must have felt much like me as I waited to see Jesus's reaction to me walking down the beach to meet Him.

Much like the story, I wasn't met with a lecture, just redemption—restoration, beauty, and innocence. Finally, after almost 35 years, I could breathe deeply, and I knew I was home. Home with God, my shame not separating me from His embrace. Home with my life and the beauty that He had made of it. Home with myself. This wasn't the life I had dreamed of when I was small, but I wasn't going to hide in shame the beauty that He had brought so perfectly through my ashes.

12

God's Miracle

I was at home, and I was living in a deep state of peace. I was rebuilding the ruins of my heart, and it felt like it never had before. Where my emotions and heart always felt like a roller-coaster, I was now steady. Much to my surprise, it wasn't nearly as hard as I would have imagined it to be. It simply took surrendering to my old feelings and not being ruled by them, then realizing that I had a choice of what emotions I chose.

Only a few months after my encounter with Jesus on the beach through Ravi's calls, I found myself in such a tender, thankful place. We had a beautiful life, a life I was often surprised to find myself living. My husband and I were making huge strides in our marriage, and our four children were thriving in their own lives. My walk with the Lord was changing daily. I was truly learning who I was created to be by the one who created me, and it felt so good!

Our youngest was almost four, and we were once again in debate season over whether or not we were going to have any more children. Shane had an appointment to get "fixed" a couple of times, but it just didn't seem right—too rushed, not enough prayer! So, we did what we had done the last two times. We both made our best arguments for why or why not. We didn't really have anything to go off rather than our own thoughts and emotions, so every conversation began feeling more and more strained.

I was 37 and knew I didn't want to be having babies into my 40s, and the gap between youngest and oldest was quickly growing. The clock was ticking, and I just wanted closure on this topic, one way or the other.

One afternoon we had a bit of an "oops," and both of us were convinced this was it. We both panicked a bit, but deep down, I was so excited but had to hold the excitement in (again), as Shane wasn't excited. All the same, emotions returned. He felt he had lost again and wasn't happy about it. Over the next few weeks, his heart calmed down, and he was okay with whatever the results turned out to be. It wasn't that he wasn't an amazing father or that he didn't love our children dearly. He was just an only child and only really ever expected to have zero or one child, not four moving on to five.

Shane was away for work when I started my period two days early. I was in shock and disbelief. Not only had we been convinced I was pregnant based upon our actions, but my heart was fully engaged in this latest "oops." I couldn't even call Shane to tell him. I couldn't stand the idea that his voice may sound like relief as mine would reflect my brokenness. I felt silly mourning something that was never mine. I felt silly explaining to anyone my pain in not having more children. Most people looked at us as crazy for already having four children or very blessed to have four. My heart was often misunderstood as not being satisfied. I just loved being a mom! I loved every part of it, and the idea that my season of not having little ones anymore was close was very hard to grasp. I would often joke that I would have babies until my body couldn't anymore. I just loved it all so much. What a blessing to be trusted with such a gift as raising children.

I sat in silence for days. I couldn't even admit how disappointed I was until one morning, as I sat with my mom, I broke down. I felt silly. Here I was crying over something that wasn't even happening, yet my heart felt a deep loss as if it was always mine to be had. She sat and prayed for me as I cried and offered some good advice that made sense but was nothing I wanted to hear. She suggested sitting down and dreaming some new dreams. What might the next chapter look like? What might I love to explore next? I angrily pushed back, not at her but at the notion that anything else could replace this desire. I didn't want another chapter; I liked this one just fine. I was good at this one, and I loved this one. How could God expect me to turn the page?

It felt hopeless to cry. Even to express to another human how I was feeling felt off. I tried confiding in my mom, in my best friend, and nothing was easing the pain. So, a day before my husband returned from his trip, I knew I needed to gain some composure. Otherwise, it was going to be hard not to want to blame him for my pain. I did the only thing I knew how to do: I sat down at my piano. As the notes and melody played, I was swept away and soothed, the depths of me exposed, laid bare, and yet so safe and protected. I sang over and over again, "All to you I surrender, everything, every part of me.... You're love makes it worth it" (Kim Walker-Smith). I sang until the tears seemed to subside. It felt like I was there for hours. I didn't want one ounce of my heart to turn to bitterness.

I had learned many years prior that "why" is never the question in moments like this but, rather, "what." What can I learn? What am I holding onto tighter than I am holding to Him? What am I called to cling to? What will my surrender look like in heaven even if I never see it this side of eternity?

I left my whys at that piano along with a piece of me—a promise of another child. Surrender costs you everything, but it is always worth it. I didn't walk away bitter, offended, or thinking I knew better. I didn't walk away accusing God. Rather, I truly found solace in knowing that He is good, even if I didn't feel good about it in the moment.

I picked up the pieces of my heart off the floor and did just as my mom suggested. I started dreaming again. I had been in little kid phase for so long that I didn't even realize how much of my identity was formed around them and being a mom. It's almost embarrassing to admit how hard those first few days of dreaming were. Then I had a revelation, sometimes we dream, and we expect this brand-new master plan to jump out at us. Often though, it's right there, right underneath the surface. It's been a passing thought, a hope, a daydream.

When I began to think of things that I loved doing, I also needed to factor in the time and flexibility that I would need to raise my four children. So, where some things had always appealed to me, it's not like I had time to pursue anything full-time. So, there it was right on the surface one morning. I had always been active and loved working out. Shane and I had been part of supporting a friend in starting his own small gym. We had worked out there for a couple of years, and the place was founded on feeling like home. It was called "The House." I loved pushing myself, and I loved encouraging others to do the same. We had become good friends with the owner over the year that we had been part of the gym, and I had helped in a lot of ways around the place. I had never trained to be a trainer, though. There it was: a new dream! I was going to become a personal trainer, and I was thrilled. I could couple something I loved to do with hours that wouldn't prevent me from being away from my family. I started studying for my certifications needed to train and took on other duties at the gym almost immediately.

There it was. I found my stride again, and my heart was deeply at peace.

It had been years since Shane and I had a long vacation together, and after this season, it felt like the perfect time to get away to our favorite Hawaiian spot, Kauai.

It was our third day there, and we were watching the sunset from the lagoon when Shane started a conversation that would change our lives. As soon as he started to speak, it was as if he didn't realize what he was saying, like the words just fell out. And as soon as they did, he desperately tried to get them back in. He told me how much he didn't really want to have the conversation, but as we all know, that never works out. "Nevermind" isn't a word most spouses accept in moments like this.

God's Miracle

He reluctantly said, "When I was away on my work trip, a woman with a baby got onto the same plane as me, and as I watched her get on the plane, I began to cry."

"That was it!" I stared at him. "That was *it*?" I said. Shane said this statement very matter of fact as if crying is something he ever does, yet it is not! At that point, I had seen him cry all of maybe two times in our whole relationship. "You cried?" I said, still in shock. He tried to tell me he just likes babies, but I quickly reminded him he might like our babies, but he isn't a baby guy. As we talked further, we realized that literally at the same moment, I had been sitting at the piano crying and surrendering this promise for any more children. Shane was getting on a plane and crying as he saw a baby!

We both knew in that moment that here we stood again, at this impasse. The conversation that we were absolutely certain was laid to rest was yet again coming back up. Yet God has a very strange sense of humor as the details became clearer. This time I was almost annoyed. Hadn't I suffered enough over this whole conversation? Didn't surrender mean moving forward?

We agreed to pray one more time about this topic, and I told God I was happy with whatever He wanted but, truly, I never wanted to have this conversation ever again! We enjoyed the rest of our trip and headed home, and I didn't even think anything of that moment in the lagoon. It felt like there truly was resolve in our hearts.

Once we got home and back into life, I began looking more and more forward to heading out of town for training to be a trainer at the gym. I would be taking a few tests, but mainly, I would be flying to another gym to get hands-on training and experience. I was helping with the kids' schools, and I was still carrying this beautiful amount of peace. It was October, and my birthday passed, and then a friend's wedding, and then I realized what never passed was my period.

I wasn't alarmed as sometimes my cycle could be weird, and I had been working out harder as I trained more which sometimes threw my cycle off. My best friend joked about me being pregnant, and I laughed without a thought in the world. I knew that wasn't what was happening, and I knew I wasn't going to let my heart walk down that path. I knew my cycle enough to know that I had ovulated at least a week before our Hawaiian trip, so there was physically no possibility. Still, though, I was more than a week late for my period, and even Shane was beginning to wonder what was going on.

I've had many late periods, sometimes up to 10 days. Much after 10 days, I would take a pregnancy test just in case. 9 times out of 10, it almost seemed to kickstart my period. Sometimes the stress over being late and so many unexpected pregnancies would seem to make me even later. This was a little mind game I would play with myself to get my stress levels lower about being late.

Determined to get this show on the road, I found an old test in my drawer, and I took it into the bathroom with me first thing early Monday morning. I sleepily sat as the test processed, not even engaged with what I was doing, as I had done it many times before. I yawned as I waited the three minutes and was just happy to know my period was coming and I could get my best friend and husband to stop wondering and making jokes about it.

I glanced down, ready to throw the negative test away, when I saw the two lines that changed everything. I began to shake, I was so nervous; I was in disbelief! My mind was racing, and my husband was fast asleep. I had no idea how he would react, so I wasn't going to wake him just to tell him. I went to the kitchen and texted my best friend my very strange findings. She didn't seem nearly as surprised as I was, like her joking had almost prepared her heart for the news. How could this be? There was no way this was even physically possible.

When Shane woke, he knew something was going on when he saw the look on my face. He so peacefully asked if I was pregnant, and I said "Yes!" as I buried my shaking body into his chest.

I wasn't greeted with blame or accusations by him. He knew this was the Lord, and this was how our story would be playing out. He still had some concerns, but they were washed away in the realization that this baby was the Lord's idea, and when something is God's idea, there is no room for concern.

I couldn't concentrate on a thing. I needed to catch a moment to myself, even to process my heart with the Lord. As I sat with Him and tried to ask 100 questions, He steadied my heart and told me that this baby was His gift to me. He saw my heart. He saw my surrender. This baby was conceived in surrender and birthed by faith. He heard all my prayers. He felt the weight of my surrender, much like He felt with Abraham. He saw where I had laid my dreams on the altar for His dreams. He was willing to move heaven and Earth, even ovulation dates, to show me His love for me.

I wept as the weight of His love saturated my being. I had never known God in this way before. Loving? Always. Faithful and true? Absolutely. Willing to respond to my faith, my surrender. Like I had moved heaven with my own human interaction with God. It's easy to believe we are so small and insignificant to such God, but I assure you this moment made me realize how much He truly values every aspect of our relationship with Him. I had never experienced the favor of the Lord in such a tangible way.

On June 21, 2018, we welcomed our miracle baby, Alina Joy, into the world. Her life is marked by the scripture that says, "Now to him who is able to do immeasurably more than all we ask or imagine ..." (Eph. 3:20 NIV). He restored everything, and it changed all of me.

13

Freedom from Shame

2020 was an odd year. Much like most of the world, every plan we thought we had was canceled, and a new plan was put into place.

I was turning 40 and planned to fly to Hawaii with friends and family, and instead, we found a big beach house along the Oregon coast and celebrated in our home state.

The house was filled with everyone and things that I might want and need to celebrate my birthday—the highs and lows of the last 40 years! Of course, it only made sense that every morning, I found myself walking up and down the beach. I'd search for my heart rock as memories and tears seemed to flow. The goodness and faithfulness of God were astounding to me, and I recalled and allowed myself to feel deeply every memory that sprung up.

As we all sat around the table one evening, some of our dear friends from church that we were just really getting to know in a deeper way wanted to know how Shane and I got together. I felt the same tinge of panic that often came when I was asked to share our story. It was in that moment, however, that I realized I wasn't afraid to share our story. I didn't feel the fear or shame that always came when asked about my past. Instead, I looked at Shane, grabbed his hand, and allowed the redemption of our story to be the highlight of our night. It's called grace for a reason! There is literally nothing that I could have ever done to redeem every bad that needed to be turned for good in my own life. There was no way for me to earn forgiveness. Grace is freely given to cover the lowest of our mistakes. It seems like a scandal to the religious, but it's the very essence of the gospel. It's offensive to think that someone like me could be given a second, third, and fourth chance. It's offensive to think that someone like me, with my past, could lead worship, raise children, or lead others. I know who the world says I am, but louder than their voices, I hear the voice of my heavenly Father.

If I were the woman sitting at Jesus's feet, the things they would have called me would have been deserved. Instead, all I saw as I glanced up was Jesus writing in the dirt, "Fear not, for I have redeemed you; I have called you by name, you are mine" (Isa. 43:1 ESV).

14

Final Reflections and Prayers

From where I now sit, things look a little bit differently. I am a happily married mother of five, and my struggles with self-worth and shame seem but a distant memory. I vaguely recall a life that I know I have lived, but something so far removed from my actual heart. I don't believe that our struggles, our pain, must "feel" like something for the rest of our lives. I do believe that with Jesus and time, even the most horrific moments can be redeemed. The deepest cut can have the most healing ointment applied. We aren't left to figure our lives and healing out alone. We aren't alone in any of this. Me writing my story was a way to share with any person who has ever experienced any of what I have gone through that you are not alone. His healing hands and his deep heart of love will saturate your heart. I wasn't even looking for healing half the time, and yet Jesus still came and met me where I was.

I'd like to take this last chapter to highlight some very real lies from the enemy that I believed came from my own thoughts. Lies I believed about myself and God and the breakthrough that was achieved as these lies were revealed. My prayer is that the same freedom I gained you, too, will gain. My prayer is that as you read this book and pray these prayers, you will experience truth like you never have before, and any false lens of how you view the Father, or yourself, will fall off.

Love Is Earned

The first lie that stood against God and me was the lie that I had to earn love. It wasn't anyone's fault; it's simply a lie that was whispered into my ear by the enemy from an early age and was reinforced as time passed. I can't say that one person instilled this belief, but I would say that it was very hard for me to believe that everyone didn't see me in this light. I tried to earn love, whether with my performance or being as perfect as I could be in a relationship, but it ended up costing me more than I gained.

I would like to pray over anyone who is struggling with the lie that love is earned or that your worth is on a sliding scale based upon your actions. I believe as you pray this prayer, the chains of performing for love will be broken in your life. Love isn't earned. It was freely given to us by Jesus Christ long before we could do a thing. He validated our lives with His life and love.

Lord Jesus, I come before you knowing that on my best of days, I could never do a thing to earn all that you've done for me. My freedom cost you your life, and I don't take that for granted. I won't let shame or doubt rob from you or me what you did for me on the cross. I lay down the lie that says, "love is earned." Freely I accept your gift of love today. Would you reveal to me any area of my life that still operates under the lie that my performance earns me love! I acknowledge the fact that you perfectly love me, no matter how much I've screwed up, and you truly have forgiven me for all of it. There is nothing I can add to your love, so help me not deflect it any longer.

If I Get Hurt by The Church, I Have to Walk Away from God

Now, it's quite clear to me that the pain that I experienced by the judgment and curses of the pastor that told me God would feel differently about me after my divorce had a lasting effect on my life. I truly believed for a long time that my marriage earned me merit in the church. I also believed my divorce would alter God's love for me. I can't say that the pain that the church and leaders have caused me isn't very, very real. I can't say that there aren't leaders who probably shouldn't be leading in certain capacities. I do know that one of the greatest areas that hurts my heart is when hurt, offended people leave the church. While I do hold leaders accountable for the pain they have caused me, I do know that we, as the body of Christ, have the maturity to extend grace and forgiveness and not walk away.

I had a choice to leave the church after my pastor told me God wouldn't love me the same after my divorce. Those words pierced my heart and were repeated every single time something horrible went wrong in my life. The pain was very real, so please don't hear what I'm not saying. I'm not saying the pain isn't real. What I am saying is there is freedom from putting our hope in the leaders, as they are human, by instead putting our hope in God. We can get hurt and still not walk away from the Lord. God may want us to have a conversation with leaders but then bless them and move on to another church, but I believe His heart is always for restoration and healing.

I may not have pulled away from the Lord as a result of hurt, but I did pull away from the body. Which I believe meant the types of people I then made as friends, the choices I was making with alcohol, my body, and every other choice changed. I truly believe we need a godly community! If we are in a community with others that are walking out their faith, it becomes way easier to do the same in our own lives. Likewise, if no one around us is walking with the Lord, I believe it is impossible not to eventually start making choices to a lower godly standard.

If you have had lies spoken over you by the church and have pulled away from God or community as a result, I would like to pray with you! These hurts could be as blatant as mine, which are word curses that don't represent the nature of God. They could be leaders creating glass ceilings over us where they were never meant to be.

Jesus, I bring you the depths of my pain! I can't believe that your church still hurts so many people! Today I acknowledge the pain that has been inflicted upon me by the church. I acknowledge the lies, the rejection, the feelings of being unseen and unknown. Today I am choosing to forgive any leader, any church, and anyone in my community of any wrongs done against me. I ask for your forgiveness for any judgments that I have made against your bride, and I release those who have caused me harm. I break the lie that says I must walk away from you or my community because of the actions of people. I ask for your forgiveness for ever letting any person skew my perspective of you.

I know that you love your bride, make her clean and purify her, Lord! Help me to walk in forgiveness and not to be offended by others but rather freely give as I have freely received. Would you help me to speak up, communicate my pain in love, and to walk out in a healthy way redemption with any church leaders or members that have hurt me.

God, Are You Even Real?

As I told you in my story, I had this head knowledge that God was real. My childlike faith pulled me in, and I just knew that God was real, but once real life started to happen, like questions or anxiousness, I defiantly needed more. I wasn't afraid to "have it out" with God. I wasn't afraid to tell Him that I needed to see Him in a real way. I wasn't afraid of needing more.

Sometimes we can overly spiritualize our need for a real touch from God. Sometimes we allow our faith to be squelched because we are afraid to ask for what we need. I was thankful that I became desperate as a child because as an adult, I may have been too dignified to demand such "proof" from God. That is, however, exactly what I needed. I needed proof that He was with me, that He saw me, and that He loved me. Unashamedly I asked, and I believe it was His delight to show me that rock on the beach that day.

It might seem trite to some, but that's okay. You can't argue with my experience. I know that the creator of the universe reached down and made Himself real to me, and the reality of that moment changed my entire life.

It's ironic that the word says He is the rock of salvation. Psalm 62:1–2 (NIV) says, "Truly my soul finds rest in God; my salvation comes from him. Truly he is my rock and my salvation; he is my fortress, I will never be shaken." God wasn't just showing me His love, which would have been enough. He was also speaking of a truth far deeper than I even knew at the time. He was telling me; he was it for me. He would be my only truly solid ground in life. My salvation couldn't be found in anyone or anything else. If I looked to Him, I would be safe and secure in his fortress, unshakeable.

I don't know what your "rock" will be, but I want to pray for anyone who is searching for a real tangible gift from God. Whether it's a sign of nearness, the reality of his realness, or just the simple embrace for you to know He loves you and is with you. I encourage you to pray with me.

Jesus, I come to you unashamed to admit I need more of you! I can't live through other people's knowledge of your realness. I need something deep from you! I pray you would mark me from this moment forward with the reality of your love. The reality of how real you are! The reality that you alone are my rock and my salvation! Father, would you have mercy on your child! I want a touch from you that will change me forever! Holy Spirit, come and make Jesus real to me in a way that I have never experienced before.

Whether it's a sign in the natural or just a breath from Heaven, would you blow on the embers of my heart right now! I don't ever want to rely on someone's testimony of who you are. I must have an encounter with you on my very own! Jesus, I love you and just want to be consumed by you!

I Am Just an Anxious Person

I struggled from a very early age with fear and anxiety. Where our current culture may say that anxiety and fear are acceptable, I still must believe God has something different to say about that.

I don't have a theology created around my experience with God, but I do know that Philippians 4:4–7 (NIV) states:

> Rejoice in the Lord always. I will say it again: Rejoice! Let your gentleness be evident to all. The Lord is near. Do not be anxious about anything, but in every situation, by prayer and petition, with thanksgiving, present your requests to God. And the peace of God, which transcends all understanding, will guard your hearts and your minds in Christ Jesus.

I think sometimes we read over scripture without applying scripture. I could have read this scripture and never applied it. I could have glossed over it, and it never would have taken me deeper. It wouldn't have soothed my aching soul. I believe sometimes we approach scripture without the Holy Spirit and don't take in the very practical aspects of scripture.

We are told as we rejoice. As we worship, as we lift our heads to God, something happens. We are told not to be anxious about a thing. That doesn't mean don't be anxious about what you can control, can't control, your situation, your career, or your kids. I think God actually means to not be anxious about anything. Then He tells us exactly how to do that. We pray and petition, with thanksgiving, presenting everything back to him.

This is a "David moment," a moment when things seem to be pressing in all around, yet as soon as he stops and pauses in God's presence, his heart changes, and peace comes. I've always wondered how David could be so real with God and then have a Selah moment and come out totally realigned with truth! When we accuse God, we lose. When we become anxious and try to gain control because life feels out of our control, we lose. I believe the first thing we lose is our peace and the opposite of peace, to me, is anxiety.

I learned from my mom to start a thankfulness list. It's the same advice I have given to each one of my children when anxiety has tried to plague them as well. I encourage you, if you are battling anxiety, to go pick up a journal and begin a thankfulness journal. Write down everything, big or small, that you are thankful for. My kids will often struggle in finding the really huge things to be thankful for, but I tell them nothing is too small to thank the Lord for. If you have been in a state of anxiety for a long time, it could be very difficult at first to find things to be thankful for because so many years of anxiety have stolen hope, and disappointment has changed your perspective some. I assure you, though, start small, even a word or thing a day. Get in the place where your heart begins to beat with thankfulness again, and from that place, peace will flow. Rejoicing and worship will fill your heart and mind where anxiety once occupied it.

It probably seems overly simplistic, but it's the word of God!

Jesus, I pray for anyone who is experiencing anxiety right in this moment to let forth a mighty sound of rejoicing! I command anxiety and fear to leave as the presence of you, Holy Spirit, saturates their hearts and minds. I pray that where worry and anxiousness once occupied, praise and peace would now reside! I declare a new season over every person who has been battling anxiety in the name of Jesus! Would you cause their worship to become a weapon that will silence the voice of the enemy right now in Jesus's name!

God Will Use Shame as a Tool to Sharpen You

I don't know where or why we would ever believe that God would use shame as a tool to sharpen us, but I began to believe that. I believed that God allowed me to be humiliated when I was young at my first huge musical performance because I had appeared prideful.

One of the main things I believed I was created for was music. I've never been the best voice in a room. I've never carried that fearlessness that some have to perform. But if you would have asked me from a young age what I was created for, I would have said, "to be a mother and to sing." I wasn't lost in wanting to be a star, as the stage scared me. I just knew that something shifted in the earth when I raised my voice for the Lord. I stood in confidence knowing that and I believe my confidence was misunderstood as pride, and I shelved that gift and my confidence for years.

I truly believed that God punished me because someone thought I was coming across as prideful. I swung so far to the opposite side in fear I completely lost all confidence and was terrified to ever appear prideful ever again. I couldn't take a compliment because that might seem prideful. I wouldn't allow myself to feel accomplished or proud of what I had done because someone somewhere might think I was being prideful.

I know that my mother had no idea how the enemy might have manipulated her words in my life, but I do know that I am not the only person who might believe deep down inside that God will punish us if we step too far out of line.

So, I want to pray over anyone who is still battling the lie that God will punish and humiliate you if you step out of line. I do believe in consequences, but I also believe that if I, as a person so flawed, wouldn't humiliate or shame my children to teach them a lesson, then He, as a perfect Father, would never use such tactics.

Jesus, I pray against the lie that steals confidence from your children! I pray again the lie that you are waiting to punish those who step outside of your laws. I pray a new revelation of your grace and mercy over every single person reading this right now! I speak forgiveness over anyone who has led us to believe that you are an angry God waiting to spank

us when we fall rather than running to our aid and healing our wounds.
Thank you, God, that you are a perfect Father and that it is against your
nature to use punishment to draw us close. You will always draw us
close with love.

Desire Equals Worthiness

Glancing over old pictures, I am instantly transported to a different time. It seems like a lifetime ago and yesterday all at the same time. I see the younger version of me—the me that hated me—yet I can't even understand why.

I believed a lie that told me that if people desired me or gave me attention, then I was worthy. How I shifted, changed, and morphed into someone else to achieve desire started small but only escalated over the years.

It started with trading my innocence for flirting as I saw the attention my friends achieved by flirting. Then grew into changing the way I dressed. I developed an eating disorder because surely someone would love me more if I was prettier, and skinny had to equal pretty. I began cutting and danced with the spirit of death when all my to gain worthiness failed. I learned to perform for love, and depending on the person standing in front of me, I would become who I knew they would love.

The trap lies, well, in the lie. I never felt deeply loved because I was never truly being me. I was too busy performing for my worth to even stop and consider that I might have a destiny and identity outside of everyone else's perceptions of me. So, whether it's changing how you dress to fit in with a particular crowd or falsifying your life on social media. Any identity you are putting on to gain someone else's approval is false to how God made you.

If you find yourself like a chameleon, lost in the approval of others, jumping through hoops for approval that you never could have imagined jumping through, or if more of you is found in the eyes of others than in the eyes of your loving Father, this next prayer is for you.

Heavenly Father, I repent for looking to anyone else for my worth! I acknowledge that I have bowed to a spirit of worthlessness. I have traded my own birthright for the approval of man. Father, show me who you see me as! Teach me who I am in you! I don't want to just know my skills; I want to know exactly what you think about when you think of me! I want to know the worth that I carry in your eyes. I renounce the lie that I am performing for man's attention.

Keep my heart and gaze fixed on you! Replace any lie with your truth. I break the spirit of death over anyone who is struggling with cutting in the name of Jesus! I break the spirit of suicide over anyone at the end of themselves. I break the hopelessness of those who think they will never feel loved or worthy of love in the name of Jesus! Set my identity in you, Jesus!

Marriage Is Always the Answer

Now, don't get me wrong. I love marriage, but not just for the sake of being married. I love covenant more than marriage, and I don't believe you get that unless you even understand what covenant is. Marriage is more than a contract between two people. It is a coming together, a promise that doesn't just dissolve in time or with disagreement. I got married to my high school boyfriend even though I knew it was a very emotionally abusive relationship because I lost my virginity to him, and I was afraid of the spiritual ramifications if I didn't follow through on it. I almost married my first son's father even though it was an even worse relationship because surely pregnancy outside of marriage is only ever solved with marriage.

I am not advocating for sex before marriage, as I do wish that both Shane and I had the intimacy in our marriage that I believe only exists when you wait. I am, however, saying that just because you lose your virginity to your youth group sweetheart doesn't mean you should get married out of a fear of hell. Along the same lines, I don't ever believe two people should get married just because they find themselves pregnant.

It took someone telling me a harsh, broken world truth. A truth that I wish wasn't true, but it just is. "It's better for a child to come from a broken home than to be raised in one!" This was the statement that gave me the wake-up call I needed to leave Aidan's father, but if I had gone through with the idea to marry him, leaving him would have been far harder.

I want you to know that marriage is the most beautiful gift from God but should be made for the right reasons. Reasons that have nothing to do with guilt, shame, or feelings of "having to."

So, for everyone struggling in a relationship and feeling pressured to do the "right" thing, even though in truth it is the wrong thing, pray with me.

Jesus, I truly believe you know who I will marry, and the word of God says you know my end, so I want every step of the way to be marked and trusted by you. I don't ever want to make a choice to marry someone based upon fear, a pregnancy, or anything other than covenant and love. I pray right now that you would help give me discernment to hear your voice over pursuing marriage with the person I am with. God, I want you more than I want to fix my own messes. Even if it means I have to walk through a season of being alone or being a single parent, I trust that you will provide, and you will watch over me. Help me to view marriage as you do, Father. Guide my heart.

I Am Trash

If I look at the first 28 years of my life, I would have a hard time not identifying as trash. I truly hated myself long before I even was able to name self-hatred as a thing.

I couldn't see who I was because I had believed for so long that I truly was trash. What's worse is when you believe these types of lies about yourself, you tend to reject the people who might speak well over you and gravitate towards the ones that will help reinforce this belief. I wouldn't listen to the nice things people might say about me because I truly thought everyone was lying to me to make me feel better about myself. When someone called me beautiful, I thought they were just feeling sorry for me. I was truly afraid to believe that God saw good in me because what if I started to believe Him and then just became disappointed.

When you are struggling with self-hatred, believing God's truth can seem like the scariest thing in the world. Someone could tell you, "God doesn't make trash!" but until the lies are shattered, the truth won't penetrate. I want to pray over those self-hatred lies.

Jesus, help! I need to retune my heart to the sound of your voice and not the voice of the accuser. I repent for my hatred of who you have created me to be. Show me where the lie crept into my heart that I am trash and only deserve to be treated like trash. Father, I can't afford to think any thought about me that you haven't thought. This world is dark and scary without your voice guiding me, and I pray your voice would be louder than all the other ones. I break any agreements that I have made with the enemy. My worth isn't for sale. It's been bought by your blood, and my heart is sealed by your Son. Teach me to see me as you do! Teach me to love me as you do! I break the spirit of self-hatred right now in the name of Jesus! Set my heart free with your truth.

Mom Guilt

It took a random stranger to enter my home and call out a demon that had been ripping me off for years. Our society would say that "mom guilt" is not only perfectly acceptable but almost welcomed. An overly critical spirit is celebrated as we compare ourselves to people's Pinterest accounts, Instagram, and blogs.

We are fed the narrative as mothers that we can't really trust our God-given instincts and the voice of the Holy Spirit and that we must rely on the voice of others. We search the internet for examples of "winning moms" as we silently suffer the pain of comparison.

Mom guilt will not only end up stealing the joy of parenting away from you, but it will also eventually give you things to truly be guilty of. Again, if you feel like you aren't measuring up, you won't walk in confidence that God has given you everything you need to raise the beautiful children that He has gifted you with. If you are not walking in confidence, you will put unwelcome pressure on your children to make you feel good about being a mom, which then shows them they are to perform so you can feel good about yourself. Too many mothers miss out on the joy of mothering because they are too overcome with everything they aren't. They won't stop to play with their kids because the house is a mess and needs to be cleaned. They raise their voice because their children are misbehaving. The list goes on and on.

Let me give you some advice. The more time you spend with your children—like actually with them, no devices, down at their level, enjoying the things in life that they enjoy—I promise you not one day will pass that you will feel guilty. The dishes will wait; the laundry will wait. You will have years of a tidy home after they are gone. I swear to you, everyone says it, but the years fly even as the days seem to take forever to pass. Cherish your children, and teach them about our King and who they are to the King.

You are enough! God trusted you to be their mother for a reason! The more you ask Him for the reason He made you to be their mother, the more you will become that reason! They aren't yours on accident.

I want to see mom guilt banished in my lifetime.

Jesus, I thank you that you found me worthy to birth these tiny, beautiful babies. I know that I will learn more about you through being their mom than almost by anything else. Teach me to slow down. Slow me down! Teach me to become so tuned to your voice that when your Spirit is leading me to change directions with my children, I will. Teach me how to put my relationship with you, God, first so that I am overflowing when I start my morning with my kids. I rebuke any guilt that is stealing my joy of being a mother. I silence the tape that plays in my head over and over. That reminds me of everything that I didn't do for my children in the day. I will stop replaying my bad moments, but trust that you are guiding and directing me every single day. Help me to cling to you and teach me to be the mother that you desired me to be. I will not be led by guilt, in the name of Jesus!

Freedom from Shame

I almost titled my book *Freedom from Shame*. It's about a journey of becoming free from shame. But more than that, my story reveals the nature of God. It's a story of God's extravagant redemption and grace. We often hear the story of the prodigal son but don't get to hear what his life looked like during the time he was apart from the father and what his restoration process looked like after he returned to his father.

Once someone experiences the grace of the Father, they still have to walk the journey of not letting their past circumstances define who they are. There are consequences but no shame from our journey back home. It's only through vulnerability and letting the Lord define who you are that you are truly removed from your past.

This is my honest and raw look at a story of hope that shows the light at the end of the tunnel is the Father. When you aren't able to run to Him, He will still come running toward you.

I believe the one thing that will prevent us from coming home is shame. We get so lost in our guilt and shame that the idea of having to come face to face with our Father again seems unbearable! We would rather live separate from Him for the rest of our lives, covering up the shame, than to have to walk that slow, long walk home, alone, back into His arms. My journey home was long and painful. I wanted to go back to church but had to overcome what others might think or say about me. More than that: What would God have to say about me? Had I never had the courage to take the risk, this story would never have been written. There wouldn't have been beauty from these ashes, just more brokenness, and my children's children probably would have been paying for it in their own lives.

Now instead, my children's children will hear of His love and faithfulness and the beauty of His blood that washes us perfectly clean.

This prayer is for the prodigals who know it's time to come home but are terrified to see your Father face to face again! He loves you and isn't here to judge you when you return!

Heavenly Father, I have sinned against you. I have traded my life for the lies and things of this world. I have become like the harlot at your feet, and I am terrified of what you must think of me now. I want more than anything to return home to you, but I am terrified to look you in the eyes. I have so much guilt and shame for the life that I have lived, but I am ready to come home. I renounce the lie that my bad choices will keep me separated from you! Thank you for your blood that truly sets my heart free.

I want to love you with a love that is without boundary, and to do that, I need your help forgiving myself for the things that I have done. I am sorry for walking away from you, and I pray that you will help me to accept your ring and robe. I won't rob you of your reward, which is my acceptance of your love and kingdom! I love you, Jesus, and my heart is forever yours! I will no longer be led by the voices of shame and guilt in my life. Your sweet mercy truly triumphs over judgment, so here I come, Father! I'm running home to you!

Have you ever asked yourself how far gone is too far gone? Do you wonder at what point God's grace runs out?

Like the women thrown at Jesus' feet after being caught in adultery, we all find ourselves in moments of shame and deep regret. Feeling disqualified, we believe our only option is to disengage with God, but His extravagant grace enters to rewrite our story.

Words in the Dust is an honest, raw look at one women's journey to hell and back and how God's redemptive nature drew her to walk into freedom.

After spending most of her early years as a Christian, Sarah Lorente's life looked nothing like she had hoped it would. Divorced, adulterer, single mom—these were the labels the world put on her, but God pursued her, even as she ran from Him. She discovered His redemption and hope when she realized He still had a plan and purpose for her.

If you've walked away from the Lord, if you question if He still loves and accepts you after you've messed up, if you are crippled by guilt and shame, *Words in the Dust* will bring you hope.

You'll discover that when you are thrown at Jesus' feet with the accuser listing every wrong you've ever committed, God still redeems you. He still sees your beauty. He still draws you to take in what Jesus says about you, empowering you to move forward in your life.

Much like words in the dust, your past is erased with one exhale of his perfect grace.

WORDS IN THE DUST

Sarah Lorente has been a worship leader for over 15 years and carries a heart to see people set free from lies and the chains that bind them. She also releases secular music and deeply longs for the world to encounter God's love for them through her songs. Along with parenting five children, she and her husband partner together in their ministry, S2A4 Ministries, to unite and equip the body of Christ. To learn more about Sarah, visit sarahlorente.com or S2a4.org. To keep up on her most recent adventures, follow Sarah on Instagram, @slorente, and Facebook, @sarahlorentemusic.

Christian Living / Personal Growth $15

ISBN 9781954943452

HIGH BRIDGE BOOKS
Inspiring Thought Leaders

90000

9 781954 943452